This Man's Navy

From prairie fields to battleship quarters

By Melvin Beckstrand

with Susanne Retka Schill

This Man's Navy
From prairie fields to battleship quarters

Authors: Melvin Beckstrand with Susanne Retka Schill
Publisher: Retka Press,10055 109th St NE, Langdon ND 52849-9207
www.retkapress.com

International Standard Book Number: 0-9766547-0-9
Printed in Canada

This Man's Navy

From prairie fields

to battleship quarters

Acknowledgements

We would like to express our thanks to all those who helped with getting this book published. To my friends at the North Dakota Maritime Museum and Dakota Bull Session who supported this vision to publish Mel Beckstrand's journal. To Carol Fenner for typing the handwritten manuscript. To Susanne Retka Schill for her skill in editing the journal, writing the history and formatting the book. To Helen Torrance and Michael Lyons who read the manuscript and offered suggestions.

We have to acknowledge Ivan Musicant whose book *Battleship at War — The Epic Story of the USS Washington* helped supply the historical context for Mel's journal entries. Musicant's book is an excellent source for anyone interested in a detailed description of the ship, its crew and its wartime experiences. No longer in print, used copies are available from several on-line used bookstores. Other sources for the historical narrative included clippings of magazine articles found in Mel's scrapbook.

Thanks to those who underwrote the project:

Admiral ★★★★	Devils Lake Area Foundation
Admiral ★★	North Dakota Maritime Museum
Admiral ★	Veterans of Foreign Wars Post 756
Captain	Western State Bank, Ramsey National Bank
Commander	Country Bank USA, Bremer Bank N.A., NDTC, Citizens Community Credit Union, Hagel's Bar

And, of course, thanks to Mel and Marie Beckstrand. Mel shared his box of memorabilia, ship newsletters and orders of the day, his books and magazine articles, with Sue to help her understand the journal. Mel and Marie shared several afternoons with Sue over coffee and fresh rolls, talking about the times and their experiences. At 85 and 83, respectively, when working on this book, they are an inspiration.

Carl Bloomquist, Board Chairman
North Dakota Maritime Musuem and Dakota Bull Session

Introduction

A North Dakota farm boy in the Navy: Mel Beckstrand was one of many ordinary farm boys of that "Greatest Generation" who came of age in the Great Depression and served their country in World War II.

What's different is that Mel kept a box of mementoes, pictures, ship's orders of the day, and his journal. War journals aren't that common. For one, in the middle of World War II, official orders prohibited the keeping of journals. And of course, many people aren't inclined to journal. Mel says he wasn't a card player, so he wrote to pass the time.

The journal is nothing extraordinary. It is not the making of a movie drama. No heroics here. Mel was lucky. His ship, the USS *Washington,* did not have a single battle casualty. But Mel's journal is delightful in its ordinariness. It is the realistic daily life of an ordinary seaman that was a cog in the wheel. He learned to be a Navy man, learned his job, and kept at it, day after day.

Mel was surrounded by the making of history in the North Atlantic and the South Pacific. But, as is the case for most of the lower ranks in the service, he barely knew what was going on. No internet news or television those days. There were radios, but he never mentions listening to the news on radio. Newspapers were received on ship—weeks and months out of date. No, the ordinary serviceman did his job, learned the news from the ship's newsletter and from the scuttlebutt.

So, we've supplied the historical context. Why his ship went to the

North Atlantic in the spring of 1942 instead of the Pacific. Why the ship convoy turned in the fog, except for the British destroyer that was cut in half by a British battleship directly in front of Mel's ship. Then there's the battles of the Pacific theater. The battle for control of an airstrip on Guadalcanal and other strategic positions in the Solomon Islands covered six months. It was the subject manner for many books, several of which are lined up on Mel's living room bookshelf. Therein may lie the keen interest in history for all those World War II vets—they wanted to learn what was going on around them when they were there so many years ago.

We can all read about those battles, or watch the History Channel on television. What Mel's journal give us is a sense of the day-to-day life, the thoughts of an ordinary North Dakota farm boy in an extraordinary time.

—Susanne Retka Schill

1—Getting launched

Warwick, N.D

Mel Beckstrand lives about the farthest you can get from the ocean. Just 60 miles northwest of the farm lies the geographical center of North America at Rugby, N.D. The Beckstrand farm lies roughly halfway between the little towns of Warwick and Tokio on the rolling prairie hills south of Devils Lake and the Spirit Lake Reservation.

So how did a North Dakota farm boy end up in the Navy?

Mel thought a bit.

"The 30s were tough," he said. "Oh, they were tough—drudgery, poor, severe drought and the Depression." Mel was a teenager in those years, the oldest in a Swedish-heritage family of four boys and two girls. He remembers the year that the entire crop filled one wagon—that's about 100 bushels. His dad hauled it to town to be ground into flour.

"But," said Mel, "We were never hungry. People in the cities had soup lines. We were never cold. We had milk. We had home-canned meat." He describes his dad as conservative—as in, he never spent a penny foolishly.

He finished eighth grade in the country school and spent a year helping on the farm. Then in an era when not everyone went to high school, Mel went a year at St. Mary's Academy in Devils Lake and finished at Warwick High School. A good student, he was considering going on for college—even considered places like Harvard. But, ads for the Chillicothe (Missouri) Business College caught his eye. He lasted a year. "Stenography and typing and me—no way," chuckles Mel. So farming it was, working with his dad and his brothers on what he calls a "pitchfork farm."

Then came the 40s and talk of war. The United States officially stayed out of the war until December 7, 1941, when the Japanese bombed Pearl Harbor, decimating the U.S. Naval Fleet. That Sunday Mel was riding horseback on the prairie fields and grasslands, hunting fox. When he got home he heard the news. The next day he accompanied a friend in the long drive to Sioux Falls, S.D. On the way back on Thursday, they stopped in Fargo where Mel enlisted in the Navy.

"I wasn't going to the Army, living in tents and all that. I figured the guys in the Navy had a place to stay," said Mel. "And I wanted to see the world."

He went back home and within a week, Mel reported to Fargo, and boarded the train heading to Minneapolis to be sworn in, then on to the Chicago Naval pier for basic training. He was 22 years old.

With a flourish, Mel started a journal.

MEB

Travel is like a book and he who stays home never turns a page.

(All personal pronouns in this book will have to be excused, as it is about a very personal friend of mine. Editor)

The Navy is a great American tradition. This country was settled, kept and protected by the Navy or things pertaining to ships and sailors. From a very reliable source I have found out that Navy is derived from the first half of the double word "Navy Beans" or vice-versa.

Anyhow it all came about like this. I was born in a rather

dry part of the country. In this dry condition through some 20 odd years I longed for water and, to my knowledge, ships float on it, so when I learned of my induction into Uncle Sam's Army, I thought, well here goes.

The present war did not induce me to join. This was planned several months before that time. So when the war broke out December 7, I said here is a good opportunity to join, and so I did. On Thursday, December 11, a close friend of mine and I were returning from Sioux Falls, S.D. At Fargo we stopped, and I put in an application for enlistment in the United States Naval Reserve. (In the present emergency the USNR is the same as regular Navy.) My application was accepted.

Wednesday, December 17, 1941 —Arrived in Fargo. Got a room at the Gardener. Rested up until 6 p.m. when I was ordered to return to the post office. At 11:45 we boarded a pullman for Minneapolis. There were eight in the party—Sandie, Rice, Beaton, Woods, Norman, Meyers, Nelson, and B. Of course this pullman is on the house. Next morning through a wild and tempestuous night we arrived safe in Singapore—oh, I mean Minneapolis. It was the tossingest and swingiest I ever spent, I think. One thing sure, an upper berth on a pullman is no place for a sleep walker.

Thursday, December 18 —At the depot we had jiggling soft fried eggs. On to the Federal Building marched the gang. Here we do something called WAIT. After several hours our names were reached.

Into the medical examining we went, and mighty glad to move around. Strip down were the next orders. Step over here. The examiner runs something into my ear. Too much Dakota dirt—wash your ear, as he did it for me. He just about blew me through the wall with the pressure he had on that ear washing machine. Next time I'll borrow a hairpin and clean my own ears. (The ketch is maybe there won't be no women around.) Breathe hard, cough, relax. These were some of the things we did.

You know I thought just old people got high blood

pressure. But I guess I had it. So I was rejected, was I—Just then an old tar came to my rescue.

"Here let me read his blood pressure," he said. "I'm the best blood pressure taker downer in the business."

And he was. In two readings he had taken it down 20 points after three docs had read it at 154-6. Thanks to the old sailor.

Go down to room 178 with those papers and get a meal ticket. Well we went down to the N.P. depot and got dinner—to me it was just plain lunch. After lunch we came back and waited—you know, waited. At about 5:15, I solemnly took the oath to serve Uncle Sam and this country of ours. We got our orders to be down at the depot at 10:00 p.m. to get our tickets. Here three of our Fargo gang had got eliminated, it was now five. But the company to leave Minneapolis numbered 56. Another night of high sea rolling in a pullman.

Friday, December 19 —Arrived at Great Lakes at 7:00 this morning. The first glimpses of this mammoth training center reminded me of my days at Alcatraz. Guards and fences all around. On we tramped, not marched, as we didn't know Navy footwork etiquette or whatever Emily Post sponsors. We stopped at the Receiving Building. Already in the building were hundreds of rookies.

Given numbers, we WAITED around like a prisoner waiting for a death sentence (and by the way I think we got it). Sign here, go there, stand over yonder, sit down there. (It reminded me of Ellis Island when I came over from the old country.) Well, I just wasn't used to that much bossing.

Anyhow in the beantime, I mean meantime, it turned out to be chow time. I didn't know food was so necessary but to see them run to the mess halls was quite the thing, and when you did get there you just stood around and waited. I believe the lines were a quarter of a mile long. It seemed like we would never fill our stomachs. Finally, however, we were shuffled up to the bean stand. You see we had a tray. It had six sections and certain grub was scooped in each compartment. At first I really didn't know how to hold this tray but I soon learned. We carry the cutlery in our upper left hand pocket. Quite a system I thought. In fact everything worked in amazing efficiency.

Then we marched over to the receiving station again. Here we got some more orders.

All of a sudden I heard a bugle sound, everyone arose and stood at attention. I didn't know what for, but I stood up anyhow. Then in walked the bugler. Well, I said, I don't know why I should stand for him. But I soon learned, for in walked the most "gold braids" I ever saw at one time. With them was Senator Taft of Ohio.[1]

Finally we marched into a big room. In this room there was squares with numbers. Into these squares went our tiring gang.

"Now then," said the Chief, "You may keep toothbrushes, safety razors, shaving cream and other minor necessities—no glassware, not even shaving lotion or your best girl encased in glass. Break the glass then you can keep her."

Then we shed the rest of our only personal belongings and set them in a square. Into a box we put them and shipped them COD to Pop at home. Here I was with a toothbrush and a razor walking around nude. Well that was a long tiresome afternoon. Then we went in to shower—thoroughly. Upstairs for a rigid physical examination, and I mean rigid. If your little toe wasn't laying exactly right against the next one, they couldn't use you. We marched before old docs and they really eyed us up. Lined up for some calisthetics or something of that sort. To get that blasted blood pressure up, I guess, because I went in and the old vet shook his head.

"Too excited, I guess," he said, "Go out and rest a bit."

Well I made it the next time. Then a sample of blood, TB test, and we lined up for our Navy regalia. Mind you, all this time we were in the "raw". This was about 5 p.m. Well I got all my clothes OK. But we had to have them stenciled. Well you know this is war time, and sometimes blackouts are in vogue. And of all times, it came now. Here I was hungry, "ill clad" and fairly chilly. After about one hour, I guess, the lights came on. I was branded and we went down to mess. It was then only 8:30. I got my bedding and made my bunk at Building E right in the hallway (Great Lakes). This was a fairly restful night.

Saturday, December 20 —All hands out 0530. Breakfast, general cleaning of barracks. Also, lessons in rolling sea bags and bedding. Finally noon wore around again. After this we went into paradise. We lined up alphabetically and got several shots in the arms—they don't hurt one, do they—not yet anyway.

Company 237 to Navy Pier in Chicago. Well we got our belongings together, boarded a seven car special elevated. Passed through Evanston and Norwestern U on way down here, also Loyola (of Chicago). Everybody looks at us. Some smile, some don't give a hoot, and the more patriotic cheer us on.

THE LINE THAT NOBODY'S BEEN CAUGHT DRAGGING IN YET !

Frank Carlson

We arrive here about sundown. We mush on down this long pier into our barracks and wait for our bags which come by truck. Then we make our beds, get mustered, and are formed into our new company—18. I get in bunks with Barnaby —Michigan, Hally Beaton—Fargo, Bearness—Indiana, Barkovich—Milwaukee and another Indiana fellow. Write a few letters and roll in.

Sunday, December 21 — Not much happening today. Write a few letters, get real haircut, sorta freakish-like. There is no choice, however. I quit writing letters because stamps only cost 10 cents each.[2] Canteen is not open on Sundays.

Monday, December 22 —Today is a real tiring day. Rolled up our entire outfit in good seagoing fashion—I hope. You see they haven't been officially inspected yet. Some drilling, but restricted because of rain. Saw ship come into pier, sort of exciting. But I'd be a lot of help on board, wouldn't I? Well them fellows learned, didn't they? Still no stamps (price going up).

Tuesday, December 23 —Heavy drilling all day. Get first guard duty assignment. Canteen open, and boy we get stamps. But still no mail from Dakota.

It doesn't seem like the day before Christmas Eve but it is. I guess my right arm is getting pretty sore by now. I have also developed a pretty bad cold, but I don't want to go to sick bay for fear I'll miss drills, and I'm not too good at them now. I guess I'll recover OK.

The old Admiral tells us to dress neater. Well these outfits we got pick up everything that flies in the air — and stuff that doesn't, too. The material is just like stuff I had in a suit when I was a little chap which was always as fuzzy as a peach. Fuzzy or no fuzz, we have to keep them clean now.

Today we are issued some supplies. Sailor's Bible it is called, and I'll have to work over two days to pay for it. Then we got shoe polish, toothbrush, paste, and Lux, of all things, for a sailor — especially when I'm so used to P & G.[3] Still no mail.

Wednesday, December 24 — I can now easily figure out

where beans got their name. We only had them twice today. Very little drilling today. Tonight we went to a get together, community singing carols, etc. and a quartet was there by the name of Commanders. They were pretty fair singers. Saw some pictures. Then we got a few small trinkets from the USO. They were all articles we could use —soap, razor blades, gum, candy, pencils, etc. It was better than nothing at all, because I still haven't gotten any mail.

Christmas Day—Woke up feeling pretty punk, but this Christmas Day didn't turn out to be the worst. Not much doing in morning. Then came chow time. It was one of the biggest spreads I have ever eaten. Turkey, and I mean turkey drumstick—no sample. I think the thing weighed over a pound, almost 10 inches long and it wasn't tough either—the best turkey I believe I've ever eaten. It must have grown up in North Dakota. Then of course a good whack of Virginia ham, mashed potatoes, buttered peas, dressing, gravy, some kind of cake, mince pie, cranberries, olives, butter and <u>three</u> slices of bread (usually it's only two), ice cream, then there was a big tray of nuts and candy. I filled my blouse chock full of them. I'll have a goodly supply for some later date.

Then feeling as I did, I "rolled in" for a while but I couldn't sleep on account of the never ending cursing, yelling and gabbing. Anyway, I didn't go for supper. I just ate an orange. But they had ice cream, so I guess I should of went. But when I heard they were going over to the gym, I got up and put on my white "girl's" tennis shoes and went over on the other side of the pier. I really showed them how North Dakota basketball was played—but I guess I didn't impress them any. Anyhow, I came out with a skinned cheek and minus my vaccination scab. I suppose I will cough my lungs out tonight, but I feel OK now. It has been raining here again today so I guess the mail trains were delayed because I didn't get any.

Friday, December 26 — Just routine again today. The drilling is getting more interesting every day. I can at least keep in step now, but as yet I haven't mastered the "about face".

Then too, I'm studying out of my Blue Jacket's Manual. It is a fairly comprehensive outline of Naval strategy written by an authority at Annapolis. I guess he's been in them for a few years the way he talks. Anyway, there is stuff in there that I never knew before. And I'm a sailor, I thought.

I can hear the refrains of "God Bless America" from my lofty bed. You know these beds would be terrific if a person walked in his sleep. I'm glad I'm not usually in that habit. Well no more letters will be written from this corner until I get some.

Good night owl.

Saturday, December 27—Today is Saturday, and believe me it was started out in real Navy tradition. We had beans for breakfast. Navy beans you know. After chow we lined up for a shot in the arm I'll not soon forget. I retired a while this afternoon to rest up a little, but there was so much noise I couldn't do any relaxing. My left arm is almost completely paralyzed. It takes me just twice as long to do anything. And of all things, I go on guard duty at 1800[4]. I don't know how I'll make out. If I collapse you'll hear about it I suppose. Then not to help matters any, I still have that never leaving head cold—also there wasn't any mail. Am I or am I not a disgusted sailor?

Sunday—That guard I had tonight was a corker. It seems that an epidemic had started. They carried 13 men out of our company to sick bay. To me, as I was on duty, it wasn't a very heartening sight. I sometimes wished I could get carried out like that. But I'm glad I'm still hanging on.

Sunday, December 28—Gone is another day. If we didn't know the day, you couldn't tell it by the routine from day to day. Sunday is no different than the rest. They have only as yet two kinds of church services, and I don't belong to either, so I content myself loitering around on the bunks. (On Sunday we get to lay on beds, provided the hammock cover is over the spring.) I see there is a shipment of guns and bayonets against the bulkhead in the next barrack, so I suppose we'll start drills with the rifles soon.

The morale is up somewhat from last night's "sick bay epidemic." Everyone seems to be in good spirits. We have a good chap right across the aisle from me. He is the butt of many a joke. Just a few minutes ago he was undressed and ready for bed. Confident and sober (that's hard for me), I walked up to him and asked him if he wasn't "going to the show."

Said he, "I didn't know there was one. Are the rest of the fellows going?"

"Sure," I said, "you better hurry."

Hurry he did—and I mean putting on all the Navy rookie regalia is no simple job. Anyway he got done and hastened up to the A.C.P.O. (Ass't. Chief Petty Officer).

"When does it start?"

"What start," exclaimed A.C.P.O.

"The show," said our good Indiana Hoosier.

"Why, there is no show—run along to bed."

He came back and found our gang hysterical. He then sauntered off to bed and now he's deeply engrossed in his Blue Jacket's Manual none the worse for the joke. As the mail wasn't delivered (some tie up somewhere) today, I didn't feel so bad for not getting any mail. New Year's is almost here, but I've already passed one resolution—no more letter writing for me til I get some mail.

Monday, December 29 —Today we were issued rifles and bayonets. The rifles are for training only, as they are the 1903 Springfield—very inadequate, I'd say, for modern warfare. We also had a very thorough drill in handling it.

At 1:30 our company took an IQ test. It was a stickler—so easy in places it was hard. Here's one of the questions. Joe is taller than Jack. Ned is shorter than Paul. Jim is shorter than Joe. Bill is taller than Pete. Who is the second tallest boy? There were 100 questions. I only completed 96. As yet I don't know how I did.

(Later - 86%, 1/3/42.)

It is one of five tests we'll receive to determine trade school talent. The report is that at present trade school requirements are exceedingly high as schools are overcrowded. Evidently they are short of seamen.

And mind you, I received mail today. A package from an old acquaintance, (V.B.J). A picture of two favorite cousins, a letter from another charming cousin (F.V.B.) and a letter from brother John. I read them several times, as it is now almost two weeks since I left.

Last night there was a regular barnyard circus around here. But it was short lived. In no time the guard ordered them down and dressed. For an hour they stood along their bunks at attention.

Tuesday, December 30 —I really had a surprise today. I got a large box in the mail—from Chicago. And I don't know very many people in Chicago. Furthermore, I know they wouldn't send me any such package. It contained almost everything in the line of chow. Figs, dates, jellies, jams, cheese, spreads, candy, shelled nuts, crackers, olives, etc. They stood about 10 deep around me when I opened it. A real American patriot sent it—that's my opinion. We also had today a very thorough drilling in the use of firearms.

Well, I guess mail has finally come my way. But still none from home.

Wednesday, December 31 —And so today is the death of old man '41. There was no drilling on the program today. Instead we listened to lectures, etc. This morning we were given timely pointers for boarding ship. Be clean, learn quickly, obedient, willing, cheerful, and ability to carry out orders. These mastered you will get along OK. I hope this sailor knows how to do it.

Then this afternoon we were given pointers on health. Keep clean—clothes, body, etc. He especially stressed social diseases. He said when you are on leave do not expose yourself, and if one does to take every precaution to clean yourself up. I think a lot of the fellows need such advice. Then we were given applications for insurance. If I could afford it I'd take out $6000, one grand for each of the family—maybe I will.

Again the Indiana fellow looms into the laffter column. They have been giving fellows the hot foot all day. The Indiana feller almost burned his shoes off him, poor kid. He takes it all good naturedly, though. Today we got fairly authentic word that we were pulling out of here in 10 days, possibly to sea.

Thursday, January 1 —Nothing much doing except it's New Year's. No mail delivered making it a pretty glum day.

Friday, January 2—And today they shot at us again, scoring two direct hits—each arm. Mine feel OK yet but I suppose they'll be stiff by tomorrow. I hope they get done with this kind of stuff.

At 1430 we took an English test. Right after it we took an O'Rourke Mechnical Aptitude Test. It covered anything mechanical as well as electrical pretty thoroughly. I don't know how I'll make out.

And another thing we did today—mind you, we got paid. It was only $5 and it seemed like that would help—but would you believe it? As quick as I turned around, they snitched me for $2.85. That left me a neat two dollar bill, a dime and a nickel. Just think all them thar painful shots and only $2.15. I'm beginning to think Uncle is a bit Scotch.

Saturday, January 3 —Today is Field Inspection Day. The "gold braid" went through our ranks and found our company in A-1 shape. Not much doing the rest of the day. A highlight of the day—I got a letter from home. Also a box of candy from Phyd. The admiral went to Great Lakes.

Sunday, January 4 —Went to chapel this morning, first time in Navy. Did nothing all day. This evening we jumped rope till I was all fagged out. George Washington Slade is really good. He is from Florida. Also today Ass't C.P.O. made a speech about gambling. All privileges will be suspended unless they quit. One guy only lost $90 bucks yesterday. It isn't so bad, but the whole company suffers.

Monday, January 5 —Today got a bar sewed on my

blouse. It designates Apprentice Seaman. The lowest rating in the Navy. Anyhow, it's a rating.

Five more companies came in today, a fellow from Minnewaukan amongst the bunch.

Today there was another grudge challenge. My fellow didn't win, but he won himself the popularity of the fellows. This one fellow (in fact it was the fellow who lost the above mentioned $90) bought his way out of the pier last night. This fellow reported him. Doc (the gambler) challenged him. The only way one can settle disputes in the Navy is in the squared wide. Bare fist fighting any other place is punishable by court martial and other punishments. Anyhow the challenge was carried out tonight. It was a draw. Just a few days ago Doc challenged another fellow from Duluth. This Duluthian immediately donned his outfit but Doc backed out. Duluth called his bluff. Now Doc does anything for this Minnesota fellow. Doc is generally a very unpopular fellow in the company and it's increasing daily. He is too much on glib-glab.

Today we also had another lecture. The lights are going out.

Tuesday, January 6 —Not much going—regular routine.

Wednesday, January 7 —Didn't feel so hot—pretty punk.

Thursday, January 8 —Rumors round that we are pulling out somewhere.

Friday, January 9 —Something happened I guess, but I forgot to put it in.

Saturday, January 10 — Lashed my hammock together, stamped cover—Key West Florida—U.S. Naval Training Station. Early chow, even got in before Co. 22, made them pretty sore.

After chow we were mustered into car companies, 26 to a car. I am in the first car right behind the engine. Of the eight that left Fargo, I'm all alone. Wally and Bill are still at the Pier. Then there is still Barkovich and Beaross. Well we left Chicago about 10:00 a.m. And I believe there was five gallons of whiskey, gin, rum, brandy and every other kind of drink, and boy it wasn't long before things were going wide open. Gambling and drinking. There'll be plenty of sick Yanks by morning—also lots of glummers on the glimmers.

Well we rolled on through Indianapolis, Indiana and at present are at Louisville at 10:30 p.m. E.S.T. I don't know where we'll be when I wake up. It'll be south anyway. It was 10 below in Chicago when we left, and now in Louisville there is more snow than I've seen this winter.

Good night Louie.

Sunday, January 11, 7:30 a.m. — Here I am in my lower berth looking out at the pine covered hills of Knoxville, Tenn. It has been a hectic night. Those fellows that have been sort of sour mouths can't do much about it, because there is no water on the train now.

When I woke up the "last" time this morning, a Kentucky fellow hollered, "Wake up you Chicago Yanks, this is real country."

Somebody snorted "How far out of the U.S. is Kentucky?"

"Well," he said, "Chicago is way up there in the Northwest Territory."

I thought it would be real warm this morning, but there is still snow on the ground. But the sun is shining beautiful like Ambrose said. (That's the aforementioned Kentuckian). This is real sunshine.

Sunday Night — Boy, the engineer is really hitting the ball now. About 65 mph. The whistle sounds like a bull bellering. At present we are slapping steel across northern Florida. Just passed through Albany, Georgia. Next stop Jacksonville.

An officer was just in and said reveille at 5:00 because we're getting into Miami at 7:00. They said when this train, Atlantic Sea Line, gets along the coast and he straightens her out, we'll be doing 85.

We just got report a fellow fell out of the rest of the

gang that are following in another train. He was killed immediately. Well the way they were drinking, it's a wonder no more didn't fall out.

It has been a very interesting trip so far. Since this morning we went through Atlanta, Macon and several other towns. We also passed Tennessee University, Fort Benton, and several air training bases. Georgia is known as the peach state. They also have plenty pine trees, mammies and red soil. We were passing a saw mill and the pine aroma was really fragrant.

And so we roll on. When I wake up I was told, I will see the Atlantic Ocean.

And so, good night.

Monday, January 12, Key West —This morning about 3:00 a.m. I was noisily awoke. I looked out my bunk to see the remains of a derailed pullman. It was rumored that the "broken" soil was for our train. Luckily, we were three hours late. No one was killed but I believe several were severely injured.

Anyway, before we came to this wreck, the engineer was hitting the ball over 80 mph, but he did slow down some. Well we were in Miami by 10:30. Here we stood around for a while, get the well wishing of prominent Miamians. Then we boarded chartered buses and started out to sea.

This southern clime really gets me. I think I'll buy a palatial palace and live down here for the duration. When we got here, we had muster then chow. The sun was really hot.

Tuesday, January 13 — And again at 3:00 a.m. I was awakened. Roll your hammocks together and snap it up. Well we marched about 1-1/2 miles under tropical stars, rustling palms, to a mess hall down at the harbor. Then we waited around for while and about 8:30 we boarded the destroyer the USS *Dahlgren*.

I'll never forget that four hour ride from Key West to my new home, the USS *Washington*. I was sick, and anyone experiencing seasickness knows what it is like—you don't care if you live or die. It really is an awful feeling. Then some of the fellows who didn't get sick kept talking about it. Oh some of things they said to me would turn anyone's stomach.

Well, we pulled up alongside the USS*W* and unloaded. Then inspection and chow. After we ate, we just lounged on the weather deck until we were assigned our quarters and jobs. I got a locker, but I sleep on the table of an ensign in the supply office (and they work until 10 or 11 every night, so I can't get much sleep.)

Well we all got our eyes and ears full of this mammoth creature. It really is a wow. Nine 16-inch guns besides fives, antiaircraft etc. It takes three torpedoes to hit in the same spot three times to pierce the hull. Then there are 144 airtight compartments, so to me it seems like it's an impossibility to sink it. Then there's fore and aft, starboard, and oh so many other kinks and twists.

I hope this 13th day doesn't have any after effects.

***

And so, Mel Beckstrand began his career on the battleship *Washington*. He boarded ship with 200 new recruits to join the crew of the brand new battleship midway on its shakedown cruise.

It was just six months earlier that the *Washington* was commissioned, floating out of dry dock for several more weeks of fitting. The *Washington* and its sister ship the *North Carolina* were the fastest battleships yet, with a design speed of 27 knots. And they were big—nearly 730 feet long and 108 ft. 3 in. across the beam. The steel belt around the ship was 12 inches thick and the decks themselves were 5.5 inches thick. They were designed with numerous watertight compartments that could be sealed before heading into battle.

Just as they were designed to take a beating, they were designed to give a beating. The main battery of nine 16-inch guns, 60 feet long each, fired the heaviest broadside of any ship. Each shell weighed in at 2,700 pounds, and could pierce 13-inch armor at a distance of 19 miles, firing every 30 seconds. They also had 10 twin 5-inch guns that could be used as anti-ship and heavy antiaircraft guns, firing 12 rounds a minute with a range of over 31,000 feet. Medium and light antiaircraft guns completed the armament.

The battleships carried three Kingfisher seaplanes that were catapulted off the ship. They would land on their pontoons in the water and be lifted by cranes back onto their mounts.

There had been some political maneuvering to get those big 16-inch guns. These were the first capital ships to be built for the U.S. Navy since a 1936 treaty that limited the maximum gun calibre to 14-inch. Unlike Britain, the United States delayed ordering gun mounts until it became clear that Japan would not ratify the treaty, and that both the Italians and French were building 15-inch gunned ships. When the keels were laid down for these new 35,000 ton battleships in 1937, the orders came to increase the size to 16-inch.

In June of 1941, when the ship was commissioned, seasoned Navy sailors began the work of writing the manuals, testing the systems and putting together the teams needed to keep the ship running smoothly. It would become a self-contained small town, having everything necessary to keep a crew of 2,500 men going for a month or more at sea.

In mid January, the *Washington's* crew had been doing standardization trials, drills and practices. The ship had returned to dry dock several times to be fitted with different "screws" (Navy slang for propellers) to find ones that would deliver the needed performance.

For Mel, it was a whole new world. And not only the experience of getting seasick, but of getting lost on the huge ship. And getting to know a whole new vocabulary along with his jobs. Most seaman had two—his regular job and his battle station. Mel was a storekeeper, in charge of supplies for the engines. And at his battle station, he was one of 100 men in the plotting rooms.

But let him tell us about his initiation to the world at sea.

The Washington in port at Hvalfjordur, Iceland, 1942

[1]Senator Robert Taft was a famous politician of the day, known as "Mr. Republican."

[2]The price of stamps was three cents each.

[3]Lux was the "expensive" facial soap of the times, while P&G (Proctor and Gamble) was cheaper and harsher, used for scrubbing or grated up for laundry soap.

[4]Military time uses the 24 hour clock. 1800 is 12+6, or, 6 p.m.

2 — Shake down cruise

Wednesday, January 14 — It's a new life, it's like night and day compared with civilian life. So far I don't cater to it. Too crowded. But you can't expect Dakota prairies out here in the Atlantic or Gulf, or wherever we are. We go and go, yet we never get anywhere, that's the way it seems to me.

I was assigned to "Section S" (stores and supplies). I was mostly in getting located today.

Thursday, January 15 — We get lots to eat anyway, all you want. But I don't enjoy eating anymore. I dunno, I guess I'm lonesome or sumpin — it's not sea sickness as this crate doesn't toss like "*Dahl*" did. But it …

I don't know what that "but it" is for, because just then antiaircraft defense signal sounded so I had to snort down to the plotting room and don my earphones. I keep in contact with Mounts 7 and 9 of the 5-inch babies.

Friday, January 16 — Regular routine but it's still a nightmare to me. Of all the new terms. I never knew the

Navy was so complicated.

Saturday, January 17—Air defense at 6:15. Chow, then I put on my blues and went to the upper deck. It felt real good to get a whiff of Gulf air and southern tropical sunshine. The sun really was hot as I lay on the deck while we were cruising around. We average I believe around 15 knots per hour every day. So I think we already have made 1,800 knots. Since I left home a month ago I have made around 5,000 miles.

Then there is the thing called general quarters. That is the time everyone rushes to and fro trying to get to their assigned battle stations. It really is confusing. I still haven't gotten the plotting room exactly located, although I find it after asking a few fellers.

Tonight as Steve and I were sitting topside—starboard[1]. I just remarked to him, in all the engineering achievements I've seen, I'm willing to wager there is none that can equal this battleship in so small a space. Boy it has everything—radio receiving, transmitting, air conditioning, ice machinery, water transformers, engines of every description, barber, tailor, machine shops, complete dial telephone system, bakery, kitchen, hospital (or sick bay), besides all necessary storerooms.

Right at present we have on board 1,250-16 inch shells and they weigh 2,700 pounds each.

Sunday, January 18—USS *Washington*, in the Gulf of Mexico. Not much doing—formal quarters and other routine duty.

Monday, January 19—Today at general quarters the "big boys" went into action. And I'm telling you things were really quaking around here. They fired nine salvos broadside, all three at a time, and the old crate really rocked like some giant. She lay here in the warm Gulf waters and grunted and groaned every time the powder was touched off. Every time they fired a great number of things break—usually light bulbs. I've seen floors covered with broken glass. I'd sorta in a way hate to try to stop one of 'em.

Tuesday, January 20 — Today was pay day. I didn't draw any pay as I don't need any right now. I have a little on hand so I'll last awhile. Rumors are around that we are going to land at Norfolk the 22nd and Philly the 29th.

And talking about Philly I got into sort of an argument with an Alabaman. I was telling of his enunciation of the word Philadelphia. He said when we get into "fily" (with the real southern drawl). I said it should be pronounced this way. Then he said those #&! Yankee #&!.

I shore will be glad when I can hear something else besides "Whatcha all doing; I'd a liked to died laughing," etc. I used to like southern drawls but it's getting pretty tiresome. They're most all southern boys on board.

Well, I haven't seen land in a week now. This salt watery air is really giving me a hearty appetite anyway. I feel like eating two meals at chow time. I suppose I'll be getting fat some of these days.

Wednesday, January 21 — I believe we must be cruising in the Atlantic now as it sure is getting cooler. Also, I can feel the difference in the pitch of the ship. Everyone is talking about what they are going to do in Philly.

Another thing about this man's Navy. Whenever you hear the name Mac or Joe you might just as well figure that's you, because that's what everyone calls the other fellow. Or they might say, "That fellow standing over there with the sailor uniform." Anything such as that. They talk of women gossiping, there isn't any taller tales told than these gabbing Blue Jackets.

I saw a fellow open a package this afternoon (W. Smith, Elmira, N.Y.) and it had fig bars, fruitcake, candy and newspapers. Boy did that look good. Why even an old paper would help me. I haven't seen one since I left the Keys. You know one of the reasons I joined the Navy was to get packages from friends at home. You know, like pie, candy, divinity and you know the good things I like. So far Phil Johnson had been the only one catering to my sweet tooth. Oh well, wait till I get to Philly, I'll buy a candy store alone and charge it to Sam.

Thursday, January 22 — Well I guess the latest is that we won't be in Philly till next week, if then.

Today during general quarters, the announcement came over the loud speaker twice — lie down with face toward the deck for torpedo charge. Of course it was only a drill, but nevertheless it sounded sorta exciting.

Then too, during general quarters today I was impressed by what air conditioning can do. During G.Q. all power is turned off (lights, fans, etc.) so as to conserve it for the rotating and firing of the sixteens. Well that stops the air conditioning throughout the ship. And believe me it really gets stuffy down in these small compartments. I bet in years before a.c. men suffered below the decks in the stale, hot air. But now the Uncle has gone modern so we really "enjoy" it.

Friday, January 23 — Well, today I got some mail — mind you, four letters. One was from home, and believe me, I never felt so lonesome since I've been in the Navy as I was when I read that letter from my Dad. I really had a lump in my throat. It was the same way that winter I was in Missouri. He only wrote one letter, but that one letter really did something to me no other letter did. There's something about those Dads that is queer isn't it? They can get a feller down — they can get him up — they can be stubborn too, but on the other hand, they have a heart of gold. But that's what makes them the men they are.

Saturday, January 24 — Well today, officers from the USS *North Carolina* came on board and had inspection. I guess everything was OK. Then this afternoon the three seaplanes of our ship had a little bombing exercise. We towed a target and they dive-bombed it. It was really fun to watch. They would come swooping down like a hawk on a mouse, drop a bomb and be away like a flash. While this was going on there were three destroyers and the *Carolina* around, too. I said to a fellow, wouldn't it be interesting if a nest of submarines were around for awhile? He didn't say anything. Reports are, though, that a submarine or two are lurking around near here.

This is sure true:

> Cooties is Cooties
> Dust is Dust
> If you don't do your duty
> You're bound to get cussed.

Well, today is **Sunday the 25th**. This was the nicest day I've seen in a mighty long while. This afternoon all over the deck sailors were sunning themselves. Steve really got a sunburn today. He said my face wasn't even burned — that shows how hard I am, can't even get a suntan. Oh well, give me time.

Then tonight Steve and I went out and took in this southern moonlight and was it lovely. You can't imagine how perfectly calm — hardly a ripple on this Gulf water. Then, too, I saw a shark today.

This afternoon the Navy planes were up again, also a large bomber flew around. But what impressed me were the depth charges that the planes dropped. We were towing a target and the planes dive bombed it. These bombs go to a certain depth, then explode. And believe me those 325 pounds even shook this crate, although they were almost a quarter of a mile away. What would a torpedo do???

Tonight we are really starting for Philly. With the sis ship USS *North Carolina*, ours, and a convoy of destroyers, we are due next week in the great city.

During general quarters last night we were towing a mine sweeper and it was badly damaged. It was believed it was hit by either a mine or a sub.

And talk about my sleep nowadays, well I really don't get much. This morning I was going on watch at 0345 and I didn't get to bed till about 2300. Tomorrow I have watch from 0800 till 1200 and then from 2000 till 2400 — eight hours in a day. Of course, that's most of the night too.

Monday, January 26 — It was just a month ago today that this big lummox was in port, so you see it can really carry a lot of supplies. But we are running short of some provisions, I know, because tonight for supper we didn't have either butter or jelly. We usually have jelly anyhow. We should have a dairy herd right with us. I sure miss fresh milk.

I am down here in the plotting room doing my 10th hour of watch duty already today. I'll get out of here at midnite then up at 5:45 tomorrow again. I get about four to six hours of sleep out of the 24. When I first came down here (plotting room) they were telling me my hours of duty.

"Oh well," I said, "When do we sleep?"

"We don't," spoke up an ensign. "This is wartime." I didn't say anymore, but since then I have realized what he said was sorta true.

The first day I came on board "*Washy*" I noticed a certain fellow. A few days later I noticed him again. Several times since then I have seen him. I said to myself, I know that fellow. Well yesterday, Steve and I went up on the main deck. We sat down on a bench beneath the shadows of the big sixteens. It was this fellow I mentioned sitting next to Steve. I looked at him a long time. Then I finally approached him.

"Did you ever go to school in Missouri?"

"Sure," he said. "You used to work in the dining hall."

"Yep that was me" I said. "Boss of the glass gang."

" Sure, I remember you."

Well, we had quite a time renewing old CBC [Chillicothe Business College] incidents. I found out what happened to a lot of old pards. He was the first student I've met since I left the old campus. It was quite a pleasure indeed.

One thing he told me that was sorta sad was the fact that a fellow I knew quite well died in the first attacks at Pearl Harbor. Arly Keener. I remember he (Keener) and a couple of other fellows and I went swimming in the Grand River in April 1939, and we almost froze up. Such foolish ideas a young buck gets. But then we had fun. And incidently, there was a covered bridge over this river, the only one I've ever seen. It had square nails in it and was somewhat over a 100 years old.

When I saw this old bridge I said to myself, I'm going to take Jean out here some time. That time never came. We were supposed to go the last Sunday I was in Missouri, but I was so sore at her I didn't even go down and see her. I have often regretted it since. But then she is enjoying herself now, I guess. At least that's what happens. "They live happily ever afterward." That is, I mean, after they get married.

Well it's now 12 bells and I'm relieved by the next watch, so I guess I'll leave and go to bed. It wouldn't be so bad if I had a good bed to sleep in but I have to sleep on a table. Boy when I get out — if I ever do — I'm going to the Waldorf Astoria, sleep in Beauty Rest mattresses 20 hours per day and eat T-bone and caviar and some of the other elegant food. But then a few days of that and I suppose I'd want to do something else. That's the queer part of human nature.

Tuesday, January 27 — Oh, for the life of a sailor. Well it is exactly 0215 a.m. Wednesday morning. I am on the graveyard shift tonight, 12-4 a.m. In all tonight so far, I've had exactly one-half hour sleep. I'll be lucky if I get two hours in before chow. Talk about being "tarred". I really am. I am standing here on Computer 4^2 literally with my eyes closed. Then before I came down here I drank some coffee. It was strong enough to lift this battleship out of the water.

I sure feel sick, too, but I guess it's more seasickness than anything because we're in the Atlantic now, and believe me we are really tossing. The waves slap against the hull of the ship like thunder. A person can't go on the main deck now without a thorough dousing of salty brine. If the Atlantic is going to be like this, I think I'll hitch hike to shore. Why, a fellow almost needs to be tied in bed.

Tonight before dark I was on the main deck and I saw the *Hornet* aircraft carrier. It was really quite a looking machine. It has some over 100 planes on it.

Wednesday, January 28 — We are really traveling in style now. There are about 10 ships in the convoy — two battleships, one aircraft carrier, *Hornet*, one heavy cruiser and the rest destroyers. We had an "abandon ship" drill, too. Each of us had on life preservers ready to bail out in the sea.

About this butter deal — well we really are out — no we aren't either. There are two pounds left but they are locked up in the paymaster's safe.

Saturday, January 31 — Well Thursday we got another shot. They'll keep vaccinating us until we're immune from Jap guns at the rate they're going.

Things are really rough out here these past couple of days. We are heading north at around 20 knots, and believe me the Atlantic is really rough. I didn't think a mammoth thing like this could rock and wave like it's doing. But so far I haven't gotten sick.

We are in a convoy of 11 ships. A tanker was sunk by a sub yesterday, we saw a destroyer picking up the crew. Then last night our destroyer sunk the sub, at least that was the report. I tell you we are really in a precarious spot now because there have been subs here during the last two weeks. I understand several torpedoes have been fired at us.

Say, I never said anything about that butter that I mentioned a while back. Well, we have two pounds left and they are locked in the paymaster's safe. And we have no fresh meat left either. We are eating corned beef, wieners, etc. The grub is getting pretty monotonous right at present, but when we get to Philly they say we'll get milk and ice cream every day.

Sunday, February 1 — Well, today we are in Philly. We just arrived here a short time ago up the Delaware River. New Jersey was on our right and Delaware on the left. And by the last Sunday we laid on the decks getting suntanned, and today is like 40° below. I guess a feller just can't get used to such rapid changes in the elements.

Well, starboard watch group went on liberty this afternoon. I'll probably get mine tomorrow. I rate liberty with the port watch.

It sure was interesting to watch about a dozen little tugs push our ship into the dock. Just like ants pushing a stack of straw around. When we got in here, they secured her and drained out the docks. So we are in dry dock. I am kind of glad for this, because now we won't have to be on watch so much. All we need to be around is in case of emergency. That's why only half leave the ship at a time. When we go down the gang plank, we first salute the officer, then the flag in the stern of the ship. We repeat this when coming in.

Also in the docks they are building a destroyer, mine layer, and they are working on the British aircraft carrier which was reportedly sunk some time ago. The other day Steve thought he'd get a little nap. So he climbed up in the motor launch and sorta dozed off. Well, all too soon he was awakened. He found they were lowering the boat with a group of officers aboard.

I asked what did they say?

"They just laughed," he said. But he really didn't know what to do.

Monday, February 2—Here we are in town where the Uncle Sam sends and takes mail twice a day or more, and I haven't got but one letter in two weeks. I think it's a shame, and when I see these fellows getting packages of good stuff for the "tummy" and newspapers and magazines it makes me sorta wish I was a civvy again. I better quit this pitying myself or I will get lonesome. But I do wish I'd at least get some letters.

Today I worked in Main Issue Room No. 2. I really felt big sitting at the desk and running the place by myself. I only made a few issues, though, as business was pretty dull.

As I look under this mammoth thing here in dry dock, I really marvel. I can see her screws almost the height of two men. There are four of them and I never dreamed that we lived under water as far as we do. Why I believe the waterline is two-thirds of the side of the ship.

If one didn't know we were in port you could tell it by the chow anyway—because today we got butter and ice cream—and they really taste good. Then tomorrow we are going to have apple pie and ice cream for dinner. I saw the menu for tomorrow. In fact I can tell you our meals for next week as they are planned well in advance. Then another thing I noticed. We are going to take on around 170,000 pounds of butter, enough for three months so I guess we maybe are going in for some sort of "meanners."

Wednesday, February 4 — It's really cold in Philly today, especially after what we've been used to. My face is really chapped tonight from being outside. See, we are taking on supplies, and plenty of them too. I guess when we leave here this time we'll be out for a plenty long time.

Wednesday, February 11 — Have we been taking on the supplies! It seems that we have enough on now for several months — soap, food, spare parts, everything imaginable.

Then there are workmen all over the place fixing things up. They are putting in a demagnetizer outfit which is suppose to make the ship immune from mines. Also, 20 new guns have been added. By the looks of things we are really going in for some excitement.

Talking about food — the crew of this ship consumes nearly $8000 worth of food a week, yet it only costs Uncle Sam 55 cents per day to feed each man. Not bad considering the food — like at noon today we had fried chicken and trimmings, apple pie and ice cream. But of course, we don't get that every day.

Monday, February 16 — Supplies, supplies, everywhere supplies. One day (Saturday, 14) we loaded 137,000 lbs. flour, 50,000 lbs. sugar, 19,000 lbs. potatoes (dehydrated). We put them down on the 5th deck, three sacks at a time. I worked 'til 11:30 and was I tired, but the chief gave us ham sandwiches and coffee afterwards. Then he said we could sleep overtime, which was 7 o'clock. But I haven't felt so good for a long time after that workout. I really am getting fat and I like to work, especially outside like that.

4000 lbs. corned beef, 300 gal. catsup, 3,000 lbs. salmon, 17,500 lbs. apple sauce, 10,000 lbs. prunes, 6,000 lbs. carrots, 7,000 lbs. lard, 47,600 lbs. milk, and listen to this — 7,400 lbs. beans, 31,000 lbs. tomatoes, 19,400 lbs. jam, 21,600 lbs. peas canned, 3,000 lbs. raisins, 1,200 lbs. cocoa, 740 lbs. coconut, 2,300 lbs. rice, 19,000 lbs. pineapple, 19,000 lbs. peaches, 6,200 lbs. figs, 11,000 lbs. pears and Popeye's spinach 6,000 lbs., 13,000 lbs. apricots, 17,000 lbs. coffee besides more beans (string 5,200 lbs.).

Of course this is only part of the rations—meat, potatoes (sweet and Irish) ship's supplies—spare parts. Repairs and 20 machine guns are being added. You can't tell me we aren't going out for some action, and of a prolonged term.

Today we had a drill in gas masks. After we were in this gas chamber awhile he said, "Remove your gas masks."

We did and believe me it was strong stuff. Then he said, "Out of here, on the double."

Well I happened to be the last one out so I got a little extra. And believe me, the tears really came. My eyes are a little sore yet. Of course it was just tear gas, but it was a drill, and could be applied whenever we get in more severe circumstances. And it rather looks like we are going to tangle with some of those raiders that are waiting for us off Jersey.

I thought when we got here in port we wouldn't have so many watches but they seem to never cease, 22 to 23 hour days come too often. And it doesn't pay to let them catch you catnapping. They're pretty hard on you, I understand. I almost have done it. It's a court martial offense, punishable by death, to catch a man napping on watch. It's that serious now in war time.

Thursday, February 19—"Prepare to get ship underway at zero five hundred." That was the first words I heard over the loud speaker this morning. And tonight we are pitching it again on the raging Atlantic. We are making about 35 miles per hour at present, and the old boat is really pitching. We have two light cruisers on either side and they are ploughing through these mountainous waves like a bullet. Whenever a wave hits any part of the ships, the mist from the waves makes it look a bit foggy out.

There are plenty of submarines around but we are prepared. Bring them on. It would be on a night like tonight that a battle would be miserable, as it is cold and stormy. And to think of only the vest-type life preservers we have. See, we took off all lifeboats when we were in Philly as to save splinters from flying during gunfire. Then all the bulletin boards were stripped of their glass covers so as to prevent any cuts, etc. It seems very probable that we shall connect some of these days. I hope it isn't too far away.

Monday, February 23 — Well we had a rough two days but now we are down in Hampton Roads in the Chesapeake of Norfolk, Virg., anchored about a mile from shore. We took on 16-inch shells, and believe me, are they big and heavy — 2,700 lbs. each. They reach up over my head and I just can't get my arms around them. Also we took on over 600,000 gal. diesel fuel oil. We are loaded down to capacity. Provisions for 120 days, but I doubt if we stay out that long.

Friday, March 6 — I am standing one of those pleasant Condition III watches[3]. Of course my shift isn't so bad. I have the 8-12 tonight. Then I'll have the 8-12 in the morning again.

Since last writing we have been in dry-dock at Portsmouth, Virg. As our ship was vibrating very bad from unbalanced screws, two new ones were installed. Each one just weighs 33,875 pounds or almost 17 tons. They are about 10 feet in diameter and are solid brass.

Well, we took on more provisions, then yesterday we pulled out here in Hampton roads again. We took on another barge-full of fuel and still more provisions. If we don't get out to sea soon we'll eat on all we've lugged on.

Yes, and I have gotten some "pogey bait"[4] in the last few weeks. Things like that really go over with us fellers. But I guess you folks on the mainland are restricted as to the use of sugar. Anyhow, with that and Navy cooking, I am getting a little "expanded around the middle." In fact when reveille goes, I find it hard to roll my carcass out of bed. At 5:30 the loudspeaker blares "Up all Idlers," mind you. The regular gang get up between 400 and 500. But the nerve of calling a fellow in bed at 5:30 an Idler. That's the way this man's Navy is.

***

[1]Starboard means the right side of the ship when looking forward; port is the left. The bow is the forward part of the ship, or fore; aft is the rear, or stern of the ship.

[2]Computer 4 — Forerunners of today's computers, the huge electromagnetic computers were used to speed up the lengthy calculations of the target positions given by spotters into coordinates for each gun mount's aim.

[3]Condition III watch meant all the airtight compartments were locked down. The many ship compartments had oblong doors, with a short passage and another oblong door. The doors had four screw bolts that were locked down for the duration of the Condition III. There was one level higher than Condition III, called Zed.

[4]Pogey bait were sweets. It was a term used by the "old salters" — the older sailors. They looked down on the young kids, some of them only 16 or 17 year-old, fuzzy-faced kids who hadn't even shaved yet, who would line up at the Gedunk Stands — a refreshment stand with ice cream and sweets.

Mel and his buddy, Steve, on leave on Broadway, New York, NY,

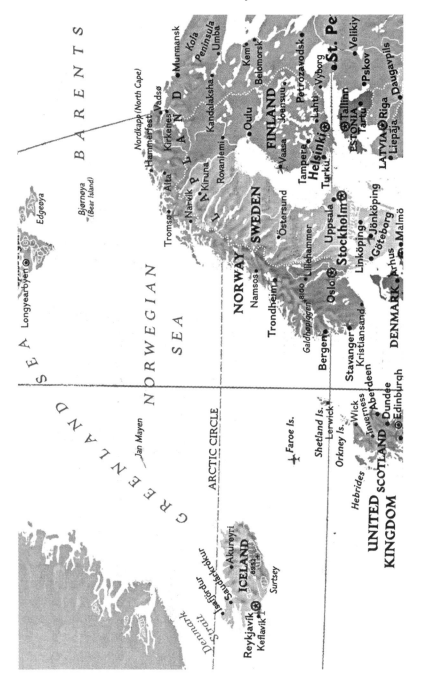

3 — The North Atlantic

The men on the *Washington* had been drilled, they'd carried on barge loads of provisions, and they were ready for action. Four months after the bombing of Pearl Harbor, they were ready to head south, through the Panama Canal, and on west to take on the Japanese. But the first week of March they left Virginia with new screws and headed north. They were on their way to the staging base for Atlantic operations at Casco Bay near Portland, Maine.

All through the war, Mel and his sea mates never knew where they were going until they were underway. And they hardly ever knew why, though the seamen's discussions around the water coolers and coffee pots — the scuttlebutt — analyzed every move, rightly or wrongly.

By March of 1942, things were going badly for the Allied forces. Japan's strike at Pearl Harbor had crippled the U.S. Navy, although the U.S. carriers that had been spared were able to harass Japanese bases in the Gilbert and Marshall Islands. The British Navy had also taken a blow when the Japanese sunk two of their ships in the Far East. Malaya and Singapore surrendered February 15. U.S. forces in the Philippines put up a fight before being overrun. February 27, a combined Allied fleet — American, British, Dutch, Australian — was annihilated at the Battle of the Java Sea. The first week of March, the Dutch colonies surrendered, giving the Japanese a near self-sufficiency in oil, rubber, tin and rice.

The Japanese looked to give Britain's Far East empire a crippling blow. Ceylon, on the tip of India, was a possibility. Another concern was the chance Japan would look to Madagascar, to give Japan control of the waters at the back door to the Suez Canal. But that objective would require informing the Germans. The message to Germany was intercepted, and the British asked the Americans for help. The plan was hatched to send a U.S. carrier group to Britain's Home Fleet base on the northern islands of Scotland. That would free up British ships for temporary reassignment to buttress their defenses, and keep Madagascar a backwater of the war.

Thus began the plans that would send Task Force 39 to the North Atlantic. They steamed out of Casco Bay on March 26, with a contingent of cruisers and destroyers creating an antisubmarine screen around the carrier *Wasp* and the battleship *Washington*. The *Washington* was the flag ship of the task force — they literally flew the flag of the Admiral in charge of the task force, who had quarters with his staff on the battleship.

Rear Admiral John Wilcox had boarded the *Washington* in mid-December. He had a reputation for giving the people on the bridge a bad time, and was not well liked. In stormy seas on the second day out of Maine on their way to the North Atlantic, Wilcox was swept overboard. Mel remembers that day. "They called us to muster several times." Muster was the procedure where the sailors lined up in order, and roll was taken by their division officer.

"You see, there was a man seen overboard, he was seen in the water. But when they mustered us, everyone was accounted for." It wasn't until they went to inform the admiral that they found the admiral was the missing person. "I still wonder myself if it was an accident," said Mel.

After the Sunday memorial service for the admiral, the captain announced their mission — to support the Murmansk convoys. Of all the duties in the North Atlantic, escorting the merchant ship convoys of supplies to the northern Russian seaport at Murmansk was considered the most disagreeable and dangerous. Initiated by the British in 1941, the convoys were considered suicidal, but a political necessity. The 24 hours of daylight in the northern seas during summer made them vulnerable to the German U-boat submarines based in German-occupied Norway. And, the Germans had a powerful surface navy contingent lurking in the Norwegian fjords, led by their new powerhouse—the 42,000 ton battleship, the *Von Tirpitz*.

Nearing Scotland, British ships came out to greet Task Force 39, beefing up the antisubmarine screen as they headed to British waters routinely scouted by German U-boats and planes. Mel found the experience thrilling.

Friday, April 3—Storms for 10 solid days. Whenever you hear anyone telling how rough and rugged the North Atlantic is, please believe them, because I don't think it's possible to say rough enough. I haven't eaten anything for a couple of days. Last night I had a sandwich, but didn't have it long enough to get any energy out of it. A person can't go on the main deck because the water would wash you away. But every day I go out on the superstructure and view its "snow covered mountains." I hear the wind howling and whistling through the masts and radio antenna at over 40 knots. I am chilled and mighty thrilled.

Saturday, April 4—Last night land was sighted off the port bow. It sounded good to hear the mention of it. I can now well realize how Columbus' men must have felt after so many months at sea. But still I am mighty "tarred." Three hours is about the most sleep we got at any one time. "On the alert" I have found out is a real war time truth.

This morning I got my first glimpse of Scotland. Scapa Flow is the home base of His Majesty's Fleet during the war. We came proudly up through the bay—mines by the thousands on either side—Limey cruisers and battleships, tugboats and launches, sub chasers and torpedo boats, aircraft carriers and rowboats by the hundreds as far as eye could see through the openings of water through the heather (at least it was something brown) covered mountains and hills here in the Orkneys.

From each ship hundreds of feet in the air were attached barrage balloons.[1] It presented a rather somewhat warlike spectacle. After all I guess we are at war. We are but two hours bombing distance from the Nazis, so I imagine any day now we may see a Stuka, Messerschmitt or a Heinkel. But if these blasted bloody blokes of Limeys will pitch in and help we may sort of beat them off.

At quarters this morning our division officer was telling of an artist back in World War I that sat on one of the Scottish Hills and started painting the German Fleet which was then bottled up here in the Flow. During the course of his painting he noticed the water line going higher and higher. Before he finished the entire German fleet had scuttled. Some have been salvaged, but to this day there are German ships in this bay. Who knows? Maybe we are anchored on the wreck of an old battleship. Here, too, is where a German sub wrecked havoc at the start of this present war.

Monday, April 6 — Yesterday was Easter Sunday and one that won't be forgotten for a long time. Yesterday was the first time I set foot on Scottish soil. I mean mud. But it was all very interesting. The reason I went over on the beach was that I had official business — I was on shore patrol. Cobblestone walks, barrage balloons, bullocks pulling a one lay plow. And I'll say this, they were the straightest furrows I have ever seen, tractor or horses. When he finished a dead furrow it came out exactly to the inch. No turning around in the middle of the field.

The people, too, are very interesting. Why those bloody blokes, you could hardly understand them. Then, after our patrol was over, we (Mario Zanello, New York City) had a plate dinner — beans, sausage, fried spuds and two slices of bread for one shilling (about 20 or 23 cents). I guess we aren't going to stay here long though. The *Von Tirpitz* is in Norway so maybe it's Norgy next.

Sunday, April 26 — It's almost a month now since we left Portland, (Maine). And in all this time I haven't received a single letter. I read month-old letters over and over again.

Yesterday, I was over to the Isle of Flotta. We had a softball game with the undefeated Third Division But they couldn't say so afterward, we won 18-10. So far we are undefeated. They call our division the "Mighty S Div Rolls On" in the morning paper. Ours was last year's ship champions. The other divisions we have taken are "PA" and "EX".

Then after the game Zan and Lindsey and myself walked over to the post office (2-1/2 miles) and bought four pounds of cookies and crackers and downed every one of them. We also got some supposedly strawberry pop. It was a very interesting store.

About a week ago, I attended some kind of doings over in Lyness. It was singing, acting, etc. The singing was fairly good but the acting was only fair, although it did produce numerous laffs.

Wednesday, April 29—At 2115 last night we got underway. Where we're going isn't known. There are seven cans, *Kenya, King George V, Victorious*, USS*W., Wichita, Tuscaloosa,* in the convoy.

The other day Doug Fairbanks Jr.[2] came on board. He said he had "been feeding fish for six months on a can", so he was taking the *Washington* on in favor of the 30° or 40° roll of a destroyer.

Yesterday, I was over to the carrier *Wasp*. Buzz and I went after some soap and hair oil. It was pretty interesting.

It will be a long time now before we get to play any more ball, I guess. Anyway we have four straight, we beat the Masters at Arms and Yeoman 21-12. I got 2 for 3. I felt pretty good even to have played at all.

About the *Wasp* again, they just returned from Glasgow. They also were down to Malta in the Mediterranean. A person really gets around in this Navy. But no mail yet.

Friday, May 1, 1942, 5.25 Lat. 67.11 Long.—For days, things have been going on with regularity and, of course, some monotony. But today we had a little incident that is making excellent scuttlebutt in jam sessions.

About 1545 today, Friday, May 1, I went in the superstructure to get a little bit of Arctic fresh air, and it was fresh too. With me were Zanello and Lindsey. We were just standing around talking—well, we were just waiting for the word to be passed to relieve the watch. All of a sudden I heard what I thought was an explosion. This I remarked to my sidekicks.

No sooner were these words out of my mouth when we saw a can (destroyer) dashing speedily across our port bow. It soon disappeared in the fog. All during this time there had been explosions ahead of our ship. Then there was a very violent explosion. We looked forward. Debris was flying high. It shook this mighty battlewagon as a leaf shutters in a cold March wind.

Thoughts and emotions were visibly and audibly seen. Old seamen looked saucer-eyed at some of us rookies and—horrified—put their hands on the shoulder of their shipmates. "This is it. This is it." Many thoughts flowed through many minds in those very few minutes, those below decks really believed "This was it." They said down where the officers' mess attendants sleep, those darkies started for the hatch in a mad rush. It was so congested none of them got out. Observers said their eyes were popping out.

While all this was happening we were casually viewing the sinking *Punjabi*. The concussions were hardly felt, we were so taken in by the sight. Well, it was a sight. One never to be forgotten. Off the port beam into view, through a curtain of fog, came the outline of the white Limey can, *Punjabi* H37. When we first saw it, it was fairly close by. Immediately, we noticed she was listing. Alarmingly fast we came towards her until it seemed we were going to drive right into it. Well, we didn't hit her and she brushed against our hull. Damage will not be known until we dry dock.

Well, I might explain how the most violent explosion occurred. After the *KG5* (HMS *King George V*) had hit her, she settled fast. The fantail of course was loaded with ash cans (depth charges). It was believed she was severed about

20 feet from stern. Here is where these charges were kept. As it settled down to a certain depth they were all ignited. And this happened just forward of USS *W*. When they connected, wood, water, steel, oil went up like the volcanic Vesuvius. We can now just about fathom what a Jerry torp can do.

As we stood there looking at those poor sailors standing with their life jackets I felt a strange security in this great USS *W*. By this time steam was erupting from the boilers, making it practically invisible to our eyes as we passed. Not even this impeded the speed of our ship, not a degree did we veer from the course.

It was a strange, heart-rendering picture. These allies of ours standing there clutching the life line. Oil and wreckage covered the cold icy salt water of the Arctic. Even if they could make it safely off the ill-fated ship would they survive the elements? A shipwreck was nothing to me until today. Pictures and words cannot adequately describe such a sight or the heroic calmness of the men. No one was hysterical as probably would be expected at a time like this. They seemed to take it in stride. As to the number of men lost, it is not officially known at present. 202 were saved. Of those missing eight were officers.

Sunday, May 3 — At 1330 today the flag was at half mast in memorial to the men lost in the aforementioned tragedy.

***

The sinking of the *Punjabi* occurred in heavy fog. The lead destroyer in the formation spotted a floating mine left by the Germans and altered course. The rest of the fleet made the turn as well. But out of the fog, the British destroyer *Punjabi* cut directly in front of the British battleship *King George V* and was severed. This happened in front of the *Washington* which passed between the two halves of the *Punjabi*. Nearly all of the crew was rescued.

The British and Americans continued on with the convoy for two more days, with certificates given to the men on their first crossing of the Arctic Circle.

MEB

Tuesday, May 5 — We are above the Arctic Circle and sometimes we come near Iceland. Easily I can see where it got its name. 20° today. Tomorrow we expect to anchor there. We have been going between here and the northern tip of Norway. Tonight the Royal fleet left us. Where today we had 19 ships, tonight we have but nine.

A very interesting thing here is the long days. In my grade school geography I learned about "the land of the midnight sun." Now I have seen it in person.

Yesterday Borkovitch saw a whale. Some of the fellows reported it as a surfaced sub. Such fantastic ideas the Yanks get.

Nothing much in the line of excitement except on several occasions depth charges were released giving us a very pleasant, exhilarating feeling. Things like that probably go a long way in making a fellow bald. Now I know why I'm losing my feathers.

Sunday, May 10, 1942 — I was over at Falcon Park helping put up Army huts. It was very interesting work. Everything is shipped here ready made and we put them together. Whenever the Marines come they will find a very good home. So far I haven't had a chance to go to Reykjavik and maybe won't because we are starting to provision ship at 1700 tonight. We are taking on 369 tons of provisions. We are to work in three shifts of eight hours each until all is on. I see where there are going to be some tired sailors. I probably won't even go to bed tonight, as I have the 8-12 watch, and then work after. No mail yet.

Friday, May 15, 1942 — Since last I was on this page, we have gotten mail. So far I have gotten 22 letters, seven packages, and many papers. It's been just like Christmas around here. I've been eating candy until I can hardly look it in the face.

And then, too, we really have been working taking on

supplies. One night I never went to bed at all.

This morning we got under way again. It is rumored that the German battle cruisers *Scharnhorst* and *Gneisenau* are preying on British shipping. Of course rumors are in abundance in the navee.

Another thing that was almost like Christmas, we had a dinner today that has so far been unsurpassed. It was the anniversary of the commissioning of the ship.

Official word was passed this evening that we are to have a rendezvous with the Royal Navy's Home Fleet 120 miles east of Iceland.

Tuesday, May 19, 1942 — We are back here in Hvalfjordur (May 17). The Home Fleet accompanied us. *Duke of York, London* and about five other cruisers and several cans. Today I went over on Falcon Park landing again. Five of us — Schwed, Coffee, Rylee, Beness and myself — went about eight miles to a farm house and got some milk, three kroner and several eyrir's worth. It sure tasted good. I believe I could drink a couple of quarts at one time now. A fellow craves things that are impossible to get on high seas.

Friday, May 22 — On one of the freighters here in the harbor, the sailors mutinied. Capt. Hittle and 12 of our Marines went over and everything is in control. It seems that they broke into some liquor (Ambassador to Russia's liquor) and really went to town. They had the anchor up and were ready to head back to the states.

Again we were taking on provisions. I stowed coffee again, 4,350 lbs. Only 68,700 lbs. of flour came on. We worked most of last night.

Well, today I was over to Falcon Park again. This time I wired two huts. I think I'll strike for electrician's mate. I guess we are getting underway tonight.

Saturday, May 23 — At 1030 last night we pulled out of Hvalfjordur Harbor. As usual, speculation as to where we were going ran high. Well, tonight at 1800 we got the straight dope. We are going to escort a 35 ship convoy to

Murmansk and return to Scapa Flow.

We will at least get into some warmer climate and be able to play some more ball. And another thing, I wished we'd go back to the states so we wouldn't have powdered potatoes, onions and milk.

26 May 1942, Tuesday — I wonder if I will ever see summer this summer. At 3:00 p.m. today we were 70° Lat and 1° east of Greenwich, England. We were then 1,150 miles from the North Pole and east of the Prime Meridian, the furthest we've been east so far.

Last night the ships in our convoy were attacked by 30 German torpedo planes. One plane was seen shot down and four visibly damaged. Only one ship in the convoy was damaged. Anytime now we are looking for an attack.

28 May, Thursday — Well the convoy was attacked again. The report was that two ships were driven from the rest and the plane was trying to sink 'em.

It's a regular northern out today. My stomach seems to take off and then again it feels like I have eaten cake or bread made by an amateur. Anyway, it was a regular blizzard last night, and today the wind is blowing fierce and strong.

***

The merchant convoy left for Murmansk on May 20. But, with no German surface fleet movements, the warships only escorted the convoy for a day. When they withdrew, the convoy took a beating from 108 successive air attacks, losing eight ships. The German success against that convoy prompted a major shifting of forces into Norway, which by the end of June amounted to nearly 300 bomber and reconnaissance aircraft.

Meanwhile, the British and Americans continued with training exercises. The British were interested in the American's new battleship, the *Washington*. In gunnery drills, they were impressed by the battleship's accuracy, and they were impressed by the efficiency of the diesel engines in both power and fuel consumption. No wonder the *Washington* hosted several official tours and many Limey sailors interested in learning from the Yanks.

MEB

31 May, Sunday—Well here we are back in Scapa. We have been busy in our storerooms every day, and nights, too.

Today, I was over at Flotta Isle again. Ryler and I were over. We walked down to the post office and "Sutherland—Merchant" store. It was locked up. Then we motored back to "John Simpson—General Merchant." Here we bought some "dog biscuits" and orange pop. The bottle was so sticky I couldn't get my fingers off. And the bottles didn't have any labels on either. Such is the things Adolph has caused.

Tonight we had an air raid alarm. One lone Jerry plane flew over. Shore batteries were in action but we didn't fire. No bombs were dropped. However 1,000 Limey planes dropped a few on Cologne, Germany, 70,000 lbs.

5 June, Thursday—We have really been cleaning this week in preparation for field day. I have never in my life seen cleaning like it, even in the most scrupulous homes. Then today Admiral Stark, Chief of Naval Operations, came on board. We really had to dress up for him. Just think all the fuss for just one man.

Also, several days ago, we were out for firing, but the elements were too bad.

6 June, Saturday—Ultimately the crown comes in the end. So it was today after a strenuous week of thorns and briars in the form of paint brush, steel wool and scrub brush. The Admiral passed with encouraging word of approval. "… personnel and ship in excellent condition." And that, my friends, was from Stark hisself.

This afternoon we went over to Flotta and had a ball game. And we—no, we didn't win. This time they were on the long end of a 6-4 count. It was sort of a funny game. Anyway we are not in top position. Of course, the usual fellow alibis, so here's ours. Cold drizzling, rainy weather, a month and a half layoff, and the week we were through.

Everybody was a little fat, agreed.

10 June, Wednesday—After several grueling days of inspection over the weekend we are again down to regular Scapian routine. His Majesty King George was on board Sunday. He made a personal inspection of our crew and also living spaces along with Adms. Stark, Giffin and Tovey. There was more gold in front of me at one time Sunday than I believe I have ever seen.

Of course, Sunday's schedule was filled with quarters, and they were in the Blue Jackets' Sunday best, too. It was 3:15 before I had chow. Then, when he left we had to form on topside again. And of course, there were squalls every 15 or 20 minutes which made it very uncomfortable. Along with the party was His Majesty's cameramen and we had ours along with the "Life" photographer. The next day we massed on the fantail and gave him a rousing send-off as he departed for the Queen and London.

The other morning we got word that mail was to be sent to the states at 3 p.m. I started to write a letter. "Turn to" went (that is, the word that is passed to start the day's work.) Well, I hadn't finished a letter to a very good friend and was doing so when H.M. Kindry came in the compartment where I was.

He said, "You better not let anyone catch you writing a letter after the day's work had started." That really got under my skin. Why did they pass the word to get your letters written and mailed, and then turn around and bawl you out for writing? That is an unsolved mystery to me.

Every day since Saturday we have been trying to play a game of ball. Every day, too, Scapa Flow weather has hindered. Well here is the reason for this uncomfortably cold weather in June. (We are wearing the same type of clothes, and warmer, than the ones we wore in Philly in February).

North of the Azores, the Gulf Stream divides into two branches. The northerly flow, which is called the North Atlantic Drift, cleaves again somewhere between the British Isles and Iceland. The northern fork encircles Iceland, meeting the cold current flowing down the coast

of Greenland from the Polar Seas in what is known as the
Denmark Strait. The juncture of these two currents, one cold
and one warm, results in almost perpetual fogs, snow flurries
and hailstorms. As these combine they furnish a natural
curtain against detection. German raiders making for the
Atlantic are apt to choose the Denmark Strait as a gateway to
the Atlantic.

12 June 1942, Friday—Well, today is one of the
family's birthdays. And usually it's mighty fair weather.
But not 1942 for me. Chilly enough for overcoats. And we
are going north again. As I am writing this, we are cruising
10 knots northwest across the tricky tides and currents of
the aforementioned metamorphosis. In other words we are
headed for Hvalfjordur Bay above Reykjavik.

We have on board 140 Lime Juicers who missed their ship
Victorious (carrier) when she left Scapa. They were on leave,
so they are going to be with us until we have a rendezvous
with the *Vic*. They said they would like to stay on here for
the duration as we eat so good. One doesn't realize how the
other half of the word lives until one sees.

One poor bloke I was talking with today has 22 years in
the Navy. He lives near Plymouth in South England. He
has a song in this Majesty's Navy. I mentioned to him, "It
isn't only the men who have a hard time during this war, it's
the women folk too." We hardly realize the worrying and
thoughtfulness they do. Just for example his family. The first
thing in the morning she turns on the radio to see if there has
been any sinkings. She is forever fearful of receiving that
certain "notice" from the admiralty.

Then he mentioned the debris in Plymouth. It was a
year ago in March that the Jerries came over in two nights
bombing and nearly leveled the town. He was just home, and
he said they were still recovering bodies. It's hideous this
war is and we will never know the whole of it.

15 June, Monday Morning—To start a midwatch
is really a nerve wracking ordeal. This is my second in
as many nights. When you have such a watch you get a

maximum of three good hours sleep in 24. It sure will be a grand time when everything is tranquil again and one can sleep peacefully through a night without watches or fear of submarine or air attack.

We arrived here in Hvalfjordur about 1000 Sunday morning. This harbor is now officially recognized as a home port although it don't seem like home in any way. And then again it does, because we got mail. So far I have gotten seven letters and the latest date is May 11, over a month ago. And in nearly every one of these is some reference why I don't write. Well I do, but it seems transportation is rather slow and very uncertain.

Yesterday afternoon we were over in Falcon Park playing ball. It seems sort of queer to play ball between high, snow-covered mountains near the Arctic Circle. Anyway, we played the top team in league standings and beat them in a twin bill, 13-7 and 20-1.

It has been said that the *North Carolina* was a show boat. I sincerely believe that the USS*W.* has unquestionably taken over that title. We have on board, and receive visitors very often. I believe I have mentioned that Douglas Fairbanks is on duty here on the ship. Then visitors included King George, Admirals Stark, Giffin and Tovey. Then last time we were here in Iceland, we received the Danish Minister, as well as our own.

21 June, Sunday—This morning after chow a fellow mentioned on this, the first day of summer, how "perfectly lovely" it would be to pack up a picnic dinner and high tail for a park or some such remote place. Before he could elaborate on the subject, however, we quietly and politely changed the subject of conversation.

Yesterday I was over to Reykjavik. We left here about 0800 and arrived in Rek about 1100. We motored up on the USS *Wainwright* a destroyer of a late class. The hospitality of the Yaks, as they are called by the soldiers, is as cold as the Arctic weather. Nowhere else on the face of the earth have I seen such reception. The scourge of the Nazism is so instilled in the people that they can't bear an American. Until yesterday I didn't realize this potency of Nazi propaganda. There was one girl reading on a lawn there and we stopped to talk to her. All she could say was a slamming of Americans. Well, we didn't know what to do so I resorted to a little Swede. She said a few words. Finally when we had irked her to no end, I asked her what she thought of Americans.

"We hate all Americans," she said hissingly.

Then I asked how about Hitler and Nazism.

"We love him."

With that we rounded out the day. We roamed the streets as no stores were open in the afternoon. I don't understand how they can be that way. I mean, partial, because everything they eat and wear is American made and they drive cars and trucks of U.S. origin such as Packards, Buicks, International. It marveled me, though, at the handsomeness of the people. They are all good looking and perfectly clear complexions. So much for the "Yaks".

25, June, Friday— It is now exactly 0235 and we are somewhere between Hvalfjordur and Scapa Flow. That was the word we received last night over the ship interior communication lines.

The past few days we took on supplies and, of course, it was accompanied by the regular sleepless nights. That's one time us storekeepers really have a job. Also with the supply ship was mail. And when mail comes it brings to sailors joy or sadness— to me the letters were all very welcome. But to some of my shipmates, it brought news of deaths or sickness in the family. I hope mine continue on the credit side.

Monday we were out for the day and fired the sixteens— three 9-gun salvos. Things were fairly trembling around the plotting room.

30, June, Tuesday— We arrived in Scapa Flow without incident. This Scapian weather is a hoax. Here it is almost July 1 and overcoats are all the rage. Without, one is perfectly out of style, as well as mighty uncomfortable.

Saturday we tried to play ball but it rained almost the entire game. We figured we might as well play because we don't very often get the chance. Anyway, we beat the EX division 21-5. As I say, it was mighty chilly and rainy so I got soaked. I came back to the ship to a hot shower and felt 100 percent better, although I feel the after effects now.

Sunday morning I went to church services held by Chaplain Gray of the Church of Scotland. He attended Harvard a few years back. Anyway, he has our Chaplain Gorski beat.

Sunday afternoon I slept a little and finished getting my 3rd class storekeeper course in. About this time scuttlebutt began to get around. At 0145 this morning the general alarm was sounded. No damage was done and just one plane flying at 1,000 ft. elevation was reported. It was very foggy, so visibility was restricted. The Jerries seem to be somewhat scared of Scapa, and well they should be.

We got underway 1600 Monday. We did shove off, all right, but where to as yet isn't announced. Rumor has it Dakar, Madagascar, Malta, Gibraltar, English Channel, Murmansk, but I believe it will be Iceland again.

I am now on the "habitual" (it seems) midwatch — 12 to 4 watch. Whenever we get underway it seems the 4th section gets the mid. It is awful rugged out and as I see the wind velocity gauge in front of me it registers 23 knots — a great decrease in the past hour or so.

1 July, Wednesday — It is a mere 44° degrees. I have never yet spent such a cold summer. We are easing up along the coast of Norway looking for trouble, and believe me we'll get it. Already, enemy planes have been located and Nazi subs sighted. Numerous depth charges have been dropped. But as yet no torps or bombs have hit us. With us are 12 ships: battleship, *Duke of York*; cruisers, *Cumberland, Nigeria;* aircraft carrier, *Victorious*; and eight destroyers.

2 July, Thursday — We have been knocking off 18-20 knots since we left. Occasionally air defense sounds and enemy craft are sighted. Many times depth charges have been dropped. Yesterday, a British plane shot at a Jerry but it was out of range so damage was unknown. We are about 400 miles from the convoy. About 1-1/2 hours ago a group of planes was picked up at 72 miles. Our present location is up near the 70° circle about 5° west of Greenwich.

The weather is still mighty chilly for July, 42°. But this afternoon the sun came out. This morning there were a few snow flurries. For several days, there has been no night. As I go off watch at 12 tonight the sun will still be up, though possibly not shining. It seems that it is perpetually cloudy. We have 12 destroyers with us at the present time.

4 July, Saturday — I wonder what this Fourth has in store for me. I am just starting my midnite watch. There is plenty of excitement anticipated. Last night at 1800 word was passed over the loud speaker to this effect. Quote, "The admiral has reasons to believe that the German Fleet is up in this territory, namely *Von Tirpitz*, two pocket battleships of the *Graf Spee* class, and the possibility of an aircraft carrier. There is a very strong possibility that we will intercept them. Our location is 73° Lat. north and 3° Long. east of Greenwich." End of quote.

We have been going north since then and are now about 76° north, and still going north. That is considerably less than 900 miles from the North Pole. If we keep on going, the *Tirpitz* will run us right into the ice floes. 24 hours from now will tell whether it's a safe or sane Fourth — Here's hoping.

5 July, Sunday, 4:00 a.m. — Yesterday we reached our peak in the northerly direction. We were within 650 miles of the North Pole. For July, it was one of the coolest Fourths I have known — just a mere 36° above zero. I dare say, though, that you heard more noise back there. We didn't fire a gun, although air defense and G.Q. went about 3:15 yesterday afternoon.

We have been shadowed by German planes for the past five days. I wish someone would make up their minds. I would like to see an attack myself. It would break the monotony of this thing. Everybody is gunning for Adolph and we aren't in the least scared of him. "Bring him on" is the general opinion. Since the *Bismarck* incident however the Limey's are a bit leery. They remember the fight she put up.

Last night we got an official announcement. The convoy is 270 miles north of the northern tip of Norway. As yet, it is 900 miles from its destination—presumably Murmansk. 300 of those miles is through open sea. Our location was 250 miles west of the convoy and headed for Norway's coast. The idea of this is to keep between the convoy and any attempt of attack by heavier craft would thus be thwarted—that's the strategy of the thing. The western bound convey is thought to be out of danger.

6 July, Monday—Just air raid alarms and general quarters—as yet, they haven't attacked. The *Duke of York* fired by radar at planes this morning through the fog. I wish we would soon have a little action. The *Wainwright* (the one I went to Reykjavik on) had an attack as it was escorting the convoy to Russia, it was signalled to us today. The Jerries scored near-hits and the can's crew shot down two planes. 25 torpedo planes attacked, three were seen to go down, the other being shot by the *Myron*.

Earlier today we had 30 ships in one formation—18 destroyers, eight cruisers, two battleships and one carrier, also one oil transport which was refueling the destroyers.

The admiral has reason to believe that the *Von Tirpitz* is out preying on convoy ships going with ancillary craft, presumably heavy battle cruisers, aircraft carriers and destroyers. We are looking for her and every time we seem to near her the Limeys want to turn around. I have heard that our admiral "fell in" with the Limey chief. Our admiral proposes to fight so we can go back. I agree with him wholeheartedly and I hope we are on the winning end. (I just looked back and saw I had written about the admiral and "his reasons to believe.")

Tonight I took on additional duties here in plot. At the beginning of each watch Lt. Fargo has instructed me on how to take ballistic wind and density for surface and aircraft, total initial velocity crossing, handling room temp and several other things are taken into consideration. The first time I tried it, I missed true wind by six degrees. Not so bad says Mr. Fargo "you'll catch on soon Beck." (Pat me on the back.) Also, I have been informed that I am eligible for an increase in rating. I am taking the test tomorrow.

My watch is almost up. It is 11 p.m. and right now the all-star baseball game is going on in New York. I wish I was there — it wouldn't be so bad if I only knew what the score was probably 1-0 in American's favor — I hope.

***

"Falling in with the Limey Chief..." the Yanks were royally frustrated with their British commanders' reluctance to engage in battle. But there was a critical chess game underway between the British and the Germans in the North Atlantic. No ship sailing to or from the northern Russian seaport at Murmansk could go undetected by the Germans in Norway. The British strategy was to keep just out of sight of the convoy of merchant ships, keeping the battle line between the merchant ships and the Norwegian coasts where the German surface force lay waiting. They tried to stay far enough out that the German's land based planes would be out of range. And they tried to stay alert to German U-boats, floating mines and planes. The fog and foul weather was both a blessing, hiding them from the Germans, and a curse, causing the *Punjabi* accident.

The Russian forces desperately needed supplies, but the Navy leaders questioned the wisdom of another convoy until the long Arctic winter nights returned. Politically, though, Britain's Prime Minister Winston Churchill decided that the convoy must go, even if only half the freighters got through. The first of July, 33 merchant ships left for Murmansk with an estimated $100 million wartime cargo of aircraft, tanks, trucks, jeeps and supplies — enough to equip 50,000 Russian troops. The plan was for the convoy's British and American escort to keep out of sight of the convoy in order to avoid air attack. If the *Tirpitz* appeared they would try to draw her to the west in a running chase towards the Home Fleet which didn't want to be drawn too far from their home guard duties.

The first four days they were undetected in welcome rainy weather.

Then the German U-boats made contact and for the next few days there were scattered planes and U-boats sighted. July 4, one German plane dove through the mist and torpedoed and sunk a merchant ship. On both sides, the warships wanted to do battle. But the *Tirpitz* and company stayed at anchor along the Norwegian coast.

The merchant convoy was told to scatter, in hopes of creating more dispersed targets. The British and American Navy escorts turned back. Of the 33 merchant ships, 22 were sunk — pawns in the chess game.

After the disastrous convoy run, the British reevaluated their North Atlantic policies. The American's loan of naval power to the North Atlantic no longer needed, the *Washington* headed to New York.

9 July, Thursday — After nine days of sea we arrived in Hvalfjordur yesterday. It seems that no contact could be made with the *Von T*. The Limey admiral didn't want to risk a battle. Since then I have heard that the Soviets sent a torp or two into her side.

Now the talk is around that we are easing back to the states. We are taking off all 5-inch projectiles as these will fit destroyer and cruiser antiaircraft. Also, the flag got transferred to the *Wichita*. The flag is a division that contains all sides to the admiral — signalmen, radiomen, yeomen, electricians, etc.

I hope this is true about our going back, and then I would like two weeks leave and then go to the Pacific and help settle the rising sun. Then, with fall coming on, the sun will leave this land of midnight sun.

14 July, Tuesday — This morning we saw the Admiral and his staff off the ship and onto the USS *Wichita*. We are now underway in the Denmark Straits and headed for the New York Navy Yard, at which we will arrive on July 22. At least that is the present plans if a sub don't interfere — one was sighted this afternoon. It is very rough tonight — of course that is very customary for a branch of the North Atlantic.

16 July, Thursday—At the present we are 56° 24' N, 37° .055' W of Greenwich. This is east of the southern tip of Greenland. Our true course is 201°. Last night is the first time we saw darkness for around four months.

We are preparing for a landing force when we get to New York City. You have often read of troops marching down Fifth Ave. Guns and pistols were issued today.

18 July, Saturday—Last evening at 1800 we dropped six depth charges. Visibility was approximately 100 yards so we don't know how we came out. It was presumed to be a sub.

The weather sure is mild, now it is about 60° above this afternoon. Seems great to smell civilized air again.

I am getting titivated up so I will be ready to see LaGuardia when we get in. I just had a tonsorial operation, and I am getting my whites lined up. Uniform blues are beginning to feel uncomfortable already. It will feel good to get sunburned again anyway.

20 July, Monday, 0030—Well, I am on the good old midwatch again. We are in the 40° latitude—so is two subs within one degree west of us, meeting us head on. Maybe we'll see some more action.

The weather is getting very hot, 77° at this hour seems mighty hot especially after being in "cold storage" so long. Yesterday evening I went on the superstructure for a breath of air. I was on the 13th breath when Graveyard Chief MAA eased up and said

"What's your name?" I told him.

He said, "You know what it's for don't you?"

I said, "Yes sir."

You see I didn't have the uniform of the day on. My white hat was missing. Incidently we changed to whites yesterday. I look pretty snittzy, I will say, in mine. I guess we'll get in some time tomorrow. We are in the 40th° going west, two subs are reported within one degree north of us going east. Earlier today a ship was sunk within a 50 mile radius—presumably by these subs.

21 July, Tuesday—We anchored in Gravesend's Bay

near Staten Island and Brooklyn, N.Y. First glimpses of America thrill me. The Statue of Liberty looms into sight.

24 July, Wednesday—We came up the river under the Brooklyn Bridge. We tied up for about a day and now we are in dry dock.

Have been in uptown Manhattan several times. Also went over to Staten Island one night. We were looking for Joe's girl, but couldn't find her. Almost never got back. I wished I knew a girl here. I'd find her. (Joe finally located her on 47th St. in Manhattan.) One of these days I'm going to see a ball game, whenever there is an afternoon liberty or a night game.

This afternoon, I had escort duty here in the Navy Yard. One girl from the Bronx came over and applied for a job in Bldg. 3, Floor 10. You see these escorts are strictly for military secrecy, but once in a while I tried to think about the romantic mood, too. Incidentally, however, she said she had a boyfriend. So that's that.

***

[1]Barrage balloons are large balloons attached to thin wires used as defense against low-altitude airplanes.

[2]Douglas Fairbanks Jr. was a famous movie star of the day. He stayed in the Atlantic theater when the *Washington* left for the Pacific.

4 — Atlantic to Pacific

An admiral overboard, a ship cut in two in front of them in the fog, the King of England on board…the North Atlantic days had their dramatic moments, but it would pale in comparison to the action to be seen in the Pacific. But first, it was to New York for repairs and refitting. After 3-1/2 months in the North Atlantic, the crew was ready for leave. And the refitters were ready to install a new surface radar, and 20 mm guns to replace the smaller machine guns. A month later the *Washington* was back out to sea.

August 13, Thursday—Since last I was on these pages things have certainly happened. I have been home. It was a very short visit, somewhere around 30 hours, but I really enjoyed every minute. As yet, I hardly realize I was home, it just seems like a dream. Anyway I was, and am glad I went. Then I have seen parts of New York—Bronx, Staten Island, Brooklyn, Central Park, Rockefeller Center, polo grounds, ball games and some leading orchestra. It's all very interesting, but would be much more so if I had some good friend to share it with me.

We are doing considerable work here on the ship. I guess we are going out the latter part of this week.

Sunday, August 23, 1942—We left the Brooklyn Navy Yard Friday (Aug. 21) morning at 4:45. We anchored in Gravesend Bay until this morning at 6:45 when we got underway—presumably for Norfolk. We have passengers on for Panama City, so we may go there later.

Now that we are at sea again things are back to the same old grind. Last night we had G.Q. again which reminded me of old times. While at our battle stations a second class gunner's mate got one foot cut off and two toes of another foot. That is the horror of war. Poor guy. He won't have to take the chance of going into battle now as he will get a medical discharge, but I believe I would rather take a chance of coming out whole than getting crippled now. Of course one has no choice in the matter.

Last evening also after G.Q., seven men jumped overboard to swim ashore and evade the oncoming battle maneuvers. Two were caught, but the other five were supposed to have reached shore. I don't understand the minds of some men. They must be pretty cowardly. Anyway, they knew they would get caught.

Today we were issued individual life preservers. Now I have that, and a gas mask above my pillow. I wonder what will be next.

Today we weren't two hours underway when we picked up a sub. Of course we didn't get hit by any torpedoes but who knows how close they were. These waters are infested with subs. At least that's my deduction after all the freighter and tanker sinkings. Today I was on top side for awhile and got a little sunburned. I figured I might as well, as it will probably be useful in "warmer" climes.

The last two nights I slept on topside. The stars were flickering above as if winking at you. Every hour huge airliners flew over, bound for LaGuardia Airport. Army shore-based searchlights pierced the sky as a giant finger feeling its way in the dark. Boy whata life. I can really go for outdoor life and can hardly wait until I'll be able to go on a couple of months fishing and hunting trip in Canada.

Oh yes, I got five letters today. Everybody wondered why I got so much mail. Well you see it's this way — "I have friends."

Monday, August 24 — Off Cape Hatteras, N. C. — I guess we aren't going into Norfolk, where????????

Sailing — Sailing over a moonlit sea. It was a glorious exhilarating feeling, the salty spray stinging softly on our faces. That's the way it was last evening. What I wouldn't have given for my best girl to have been there. The moon laid a broad ray of light as of some giant highway meandering off to some mysteriously secret rendezvous. What a perfect target if some blooming Nazi raider been lurking between us and the moon. To give him a better chance, the black gang[1] must have started some sort of a cooking school in the bilges, for out of the smoke stacks came enormous quantities of red fiery sparks. They can be easily seen for miles around. I'll bet the Captain had a fit when this was going on — well who wouldn't. Evidently the two subs reported in this vicinity didn't accept the challenge.

Cruising in the Caribbean — 24 August 42 — accompanied with scrumptious cuisine in coordination with colossal air-conditioning.

I believe somewhere along in my reminiscings I mentioned something about air conditioning. I don't think I elaborated on the subject very much and am very glad I didn't. If my cerebellar memory serves me very correctly, I remember myself as saying, quote, "I don't (of course this was before I started using two dollar words) understand how the sailors of the old navee every survived without the *Washington's* modern convenience of air-conditioning."

Since we have left the natural air-conditioned zephyrs of the 80th degree circle. I realize fully I was just talking through my hat — and incidentally, it was the one with the hole in it and only one ear flap — and that happened to be on the north (starboard) side.

Anyway, the USS *Washington* (the abbreviations—United States Steamship) has been an equatorial desert of frothing humanity gulping voluptuously for H_2O and inhaling lustily for oxygen below 85° that wasn't there. It all adds up that the unforsightedness of the Philadelphia yardbirds in not installing air-conditioning secretly while the architectural engineer was spending a restful weekend in the Adirondacks.

I think I'll get transferred to permanent duty in Greenland where sweat glands know no work. Greenland, where one wishes he were in the Caribbean—that's the human part of human nature.

West Indies—Caribbean, area south of Dominican Republic, August 26, 1942, Wednesday—It is a very warm, sultry day today as is each day, but now towards evening gentle refreshing, tropical zephyrs bring comfort and relief to a sweat-soaked, sunburned sailor.

This morning, we received word that four Nazi submarines were operating in this vicinity. Yesterday they sank a ship down within 100 miles of Haiti. When we came through the Mona Passage this morning, we were warned of this menace. Consequently the skipper could take no chances, so he had us at our battle stations all day. The passage is between Puerto Rico and the Republic.

While I was passing through this area I thought of a few friends I have down here—over in Havana, it's Ken and Mart and probably Dick and Eve. In Puerto Rico, it's Lorraine Abrahamson. It would have been interesting to drop in for a little surprise visit, but we are on our way to Cristobol, due to arrive 1300 Friday, so not much time to loiter. At present we are making 24 to 26 knots. Our regular speed has been 19 and 20. You probably understand our increase in speed.

27 August Thursday—"How I suffer from the heat and the chilblains on my feet." The last part isn't true but take it from me, the first is. Why, it's so hot this Caribbean water steams. The flying fish are broiled, then baked as they fly through the air. As they hit the deck, they fry to a golden crisp. By this time there isn't much life left, but just enough to flip themselves over and fry on the other side. As the deck isn't greased too well, the first side sticks to the deck. Then during that final kick, he just opens himself up, and there the entrails can easily be cleaned out. Pick it up and you have a delicious french fry of finny flying fish fit for the fittest fossil of the famous fighting Navy (fossil here is used in the connection of the older men of the Navy — say 35 or over).

According to the quartermaster, we are to anchor around 1017 tomorrow morning. At 1100 today we were 13° 11 minutes latitude, 72° 43 minutes longitude straight north of Point Gullinas, Colombia, South America. We are near the place that was shelled earlier in the year by a sub. A sub was reported in our vicinity today.

Friday evening around 1500, 28 August — We eased into Colon Harbor, Canal Zone. Here we docked and took on 7,500 gallons of fresh water, as we couldn't make water for the ship of the fresh water in Gatun Lake. The machinery is just for the conversion of the salty brine — another reason, it is thought that it may be polluted. We also took on 750,000 gallons of Bunker Grade A fuel oil, filling 28 tanks never before used. It may be a long voyage ahead.

Friday night the Fourth Section rated liberty. Fortunately I am in that section. Taylor Teppetts and myself were over and we did a little shopping — in fact to the tune of $15. Of the items we purchased, one of interest should be mentioned. As I am a little foresighted in some things, I purchased five yards of pure silk imported from China before the war. At present, no more can be gotten. As to the usage of this fine cloth, I will leave to the imagination of the reader. Also for a certain distant date (at least I hope so) I purchased some ex-gua-seat perfume, the aroma is fragrantly perfect, ideal for a June evening. For myself I purchased an always desired, genuine Panama hat made and purchased in Panama. It don't look like much now but "Wait," said the señor, "until it is blocked." In the event that my breeches should ever become loose on my ever expanding bay window I "jived" myself into an alligator leather belt. For the radio or front room table, my collection contains a gaudy, but ornamental scarf. To round out the shopping trip, a few novelty souvenirs, and of course several Panamanian coins are in my possession.

At 4:00 a.m. the rugged bo'suns mate[2] whistled reveille. Hardly anyone stirred. Knowing the inadequate amount of patience of their roustabout fellows, I quickly seized the opportunity of clearing up my blankets (topside sleeping). Shortly after this job well done, I just eased back to watch the fun about to begin. By this time the irate deck mate was gingerly screwing in the deck hose to the salt water connection. Rather than seeing angry shipmates, I chop-chopped down the ladders to my compartment. I can understand, though, how they were reveilled for **Saturday, August the 29th.**

Very reluctantly this same mate gave me the dope we were getting underway through the canal. At around 4:30 a.m., the tugs began grunting at the side of the monster pushing her towards Gatun Locks, the first locks on the Atlantic side. Here we were ushered in between two concrete walls. Two larger gates closed behind us and the water began to pour in. We were raised almost 30 ft. Then the gates were opened ahead of us and we eased forward into the next lock. Three times this was repeated until we were up to the level of the fresh water lake of Gatun around 85 ft. We have a beam of 108'3" and the canal walls were around 109 ft. wide. You can readily see that space was limited, invariably causing some damage to both ship and locks. Then there was the famous Gaillard Cut, a passage through solid rock. When I read of the mosquito-fighting engineers, malaria, Col. Goethals, the French forsaking and the American taking control of the problem back in grammar school, little did I realize that when just a few years older, that I, me, M.E.B. would be going through and beholding this great engineering achievement.

At the Pedro Miguel and Pacific locks we were lowered

into the Pacific Ocean which another old salt, Balboa, discovered in 1513. Presumably, and according to "shedual," we were to take on an additional 30 days supply of provisions at either Panama City or Balboa. Neither of these places received our attention and the aforementioned plan did not matriculate. We contented ourselves on general quarters and shoved out into the night — where to — nobody knows.

Anyway we are now in the big leagues where fanatical Japs fight. Where ships are sunk. Where men are killed. I can hardly wait for our first battle. The Japs will be sorry they ever picked a fight, I hope. The next stop seems to be the talk of the crew at present — Australia, Solomon Islands, Hawaii or San Diego. Preferably for me, I wouldn't mind easing up to Cal for a week or two and recuperate.

The voyage from New York to Calon via Bermuda and Puerto Rico is around 3000 miles. We made it in 5 1/2 days. Nothing of incident happened, not even the dropping of depth charges, until the last five hours of the trip when, with land based planes, we sunk a submarine operating in the area adjacent to the canal. At this writing it is Sunday morning, August 30, 1:25 a.m. About 150 miles SW of the canal. We are now west coast sailors.

By the way I can't forget my sunburn. How it pains and aches. By consulting a map you will find the canal about 9° north of the equator. And as most of you know me, when it comes to seeing things. Well in short, too much top side and too much tropic, equatorial sunshine. Consequently no sleep for the wicked. Anyone who has gotten through the tan stage can quickly grasp my ill-worded sentiments.

Good morning.

The Red Cross rightly urges people not to send gloomy letters to the men in the services. For all we know, their lives may not be all sunshine, either.

A shortage of beef and pork is developing in the Eastern states. Alarmists say that before the summer is over many people will be reduced to eating chicken.

This clipping was taken from the *New Yorker Magazine* of August, 1942. I particularly like the last note. It depicts the horrible hardship some people are going through. I often wonder how they will stand it. It would suit us fellers if we could be reduced to chicken.

1 Sept. 1942, Tuesday — Our course since we left Panama has been west-southwest. It seems we won't get up to the west coast of the U.S. The way we are now traveling we'll either hit New Zealand or Australia — that is if we aren't stopped before. At present we are hovering on 0° which is the equator. Before a sailor crosses the equator, he is officially a pollywog. When he is over the line, only after a rigid initiation, he is taken into that old fraternity — the Shellbacks. What they are going to do to us is as yet unknown, but to hear veteran shellbacks talk, they used to do plenty.

I am somewhat surprised at the coolness of the air at the supposedly heat belt of the world. Last night it was 70° above. Of course we are entering into the winter months south of the line, similar to March in the northern hemisphere. From now on, it will probably get warmer both physically, and in the form of lead. We are now in the major league, fighting for top place.

4 September, Friday — Since last writing, through an antagonizing initiation I have rizzed from the multitudinous ranks of the pollywogs to the veteran sun-scorched sailors of His Majesty, Neptunous Rex's realm of supposedly, superior servants of Sam's service, namely — Shellbacks.

When we crossed the equator 00° latitude at 100° longitude we moaningly and groaningly were taken into one of the Navy's age old fraternities. It was, nevertheless, a lot of fun, and a tremendous break in the monotony. Everything short of priority articles were used to make life as miserable as possible the short time it lasted. It was a high school initiation on the rampage. One of the tortures, which will be longer-lived than most, is the beautiful coiffures done up in the most elaborate fashions. In short, tonsorial operations at their best. My head is worse than my boot training clip.

It is almost two weeks now since we left Gravesend Bay (over that from the Navy Yard) and have seen land but once — that through the Canal. Prospects are that at the least, it will be four days before we sight it again, probably at Marquesas Island. The weather has been magnificent. Early morning temps about 70°.

Already, we are being rationed food. Present plans are for supplies lasting 120 days. Of course, our fuel won't last that long, so we'll put into port soon, I hope. This idea of being at your battle station 15 hours daily and work several hours more is getting very tiresome. But maybe it will be worse. We'll hope for the best.

7 September, Monday — We are nine days out from Panama, west of the Marquesas Islands. At the present course, it seems perfectly logical that we won't stop there.

Today we fueled the three destroyers, DD-602-499-449. Around 150,000 gallons were pumped over. The ship's speed during fueling operations is around 8 knots; ordinarily on this cruise 18 knots. They also got a few minor items — matches, soap, candy, etc. Fueling at sea is quite a sight. The ever present swells makes both ships roll.

But to me, the life of a tin can sailor is awfully rugged. They wear the weirdest uniforms. And speaking of uniforms, the topside regulation is khaki now. At least a number of the crew have dyed their uniforms, especially those with stations on topside during battle. The captain spoke to us yesterday. He stressed the need of economizing on water and lights. Water is fuel, he said, and a few gallons may mean the difference between victory and defeat. The allotted quota of fresh water is 70,000 gallons daily. From now on, he said, any call of G.Q. could mean the real thing. Anything can happen.

***

[1]The Black Gang is a nickname for the engine room crews. There were Blacks on board (known in those days as Negroes or Colored), but in the positions of stewards or waiters in the officers' mess.

[2]Bo'suns is slang for Boatswain's, the seamen responsibile for maintaining the ship's hull and its equipment.

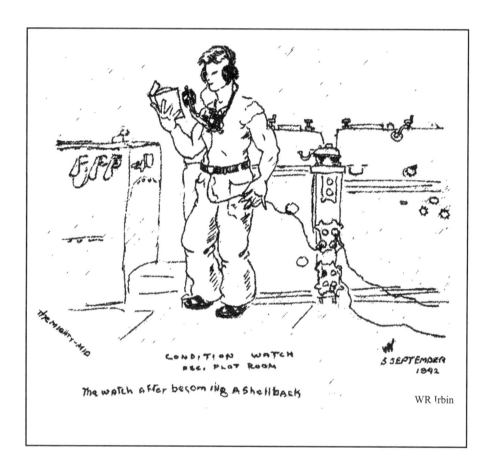

CONDITION WATCH
EEC. PLOT ROOM

5 SEPTEMBER 1942

The watch after becoming A Shellback

WR Irbin

Darken Ship

(Taken from "Our Navy" — August '42
Slightly modified by yours sincerely)

Just a song at twilight
When the lights are low
And the flick'ring shadows
Softly come and go;
Stow that butt, there shipmate!
Hey! Secure that match!
Watch your step at twilight —
Don't fall down that hatch.

II.
Just a gong at twilight (or even before)
Battle stations' sounds,
Twenty hundred sailors
Knock you out of bounds;
Who was that I trampled,
Stepping on his neck?
Give me gangway, shipmate!
That was the Exec ...
Just a word at twilight
Pointing out to him
Accidents will happen
When the light is dim;
You can say you're sorry
You admit the wrong —
But what He says
Is hardly
Love's old sweet song.

Collected Quotes

If you are self-conscious and feel the lack of poise just
remember these celebrated lines:
> When pompous people squelch me
> with cold and snooty looks
> It makes me happy to conjecture how
> they'd look in bathing suits.

—Used by Bette Davis

* * *

"I am not in the least disturbed when people regard my
legs intently. I know they are doing it in pursuance of their
inherent artistic instinct."

* * *

Old horse, old horse, what brought you here
From off the plains to Portsmouth Pier?
Worked in a cart for many a year
Till broken down by ill abuse,
Then *salted down for sailor's use.

*Ours is not salted, but dehydrated - nevertheless, it
makes an unrelishing dish.

* * *

USS, Chaplain Captain Alberto S, North Carolina said
Sunday, our last one in port Feb 14, that prayer is the key to
the day and the lock to the night. Also quoted he, "A thing is
worth getting it is worth for." End of quote.

* * *

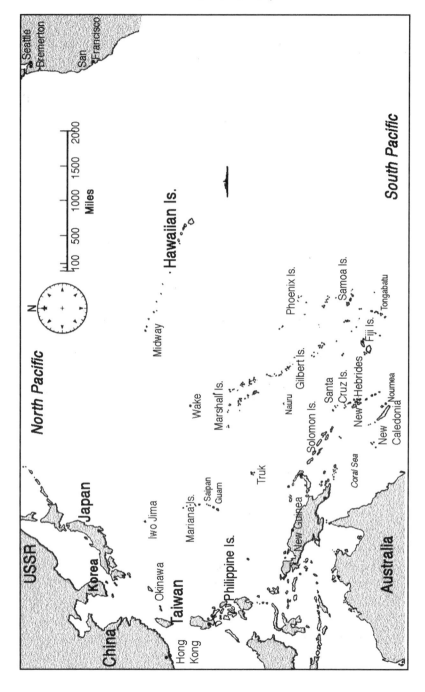

5 — South Seas

Caribbean sun, fresh evening breezes and a wild initiation when crossing the equator made the long monotonous days at sea go a little quicker. But the *Washington* and its crew were heading for far more serious waters. The war was not going well for the United States and its allies in the South Seas.

While the *Washington* was in New York, in early August, the Japanese expanded their reach towards the shipping lanes to eastern Australia. They landed troops on several of the Solomon Islands and began building an airfield in the jungles of Guadalcanal. That airfield would have extended the Japanese reach to wreck havoc on allied forces. August 8, the Navy landed Marines on the Island of Guadalcanal in their first offensive campaign. The Marines took the airfield and a perimeter around it without resistance from the Japanese, renaming it Henderson Field. Soon Japanese reinforcements arrived and savage fighting followed, lasting several months.

The same night the Navy landed the Marines on Guadalcanal and two other islands in the Solomon group, they took losses at the hand of the Japanese Navy. The Japanese had superior radar and extensive training in night tactics. They passed undetected around the southern end of the Solomon Island group, slipped into the channel and surprised the American ships. Within an hour, six allied ships were destroyed or left sinking. The Americans nicknamed the channel "Ironbottom Sound."

Two weeks later, as the *Washington* sailed through the Caribbean with its small formation of destroyers, the Japanese successfully landed 1,500 troops on Guadalcanal. They used a diversionary group to bait the U.S. Navy ships to attacking the wrong target. Both sides lost ships in that August 24 Battle of the Eastern Solomons, but the Japanese reinforcements landed. The Japanese were to perfect what became known as "The Tokyo Express"—shooting down the channel (nicknamed "The Slot") under nighttime cover with supplies and reinforcements. For the next six months, the two sides battled over control of Guadalcanal and the Solomon Islands.

Mel and the crew of the *Washington* knew little of this as they steamed across the Pacific Ocean in formation with three escort destroyers. But their commanders knew they needed training and drills. They practiced operating with simulated power failures, forcing the crew to rely on secondary systems and local control. And they drilled, turning the movements of firing the guns into automatic motions.

Firing the big 16-inch guns, for example, required well-oiled coordination. The command "main battery load" put 100 men into motion in the shell rooms and magazines to trundle nine 2,700 pound shells on their trolleys to the hoists. As the shells ascended the ammo tubes to the turrets, 54 100-pound bags of powder were manhandled into the powder cars.

Each 16-inch gun crew consisted of a gun captain, rammer man, cradle man, powder man and primer man. In the turret, the five men honed their movements. One opened the 200 pound breech, another rammed the shell in from its cradle, the third then rammed three bags of powder into the barrel. Ramming the powder needed an accurate touch—too hard and it could heat the barrel, not hard enough it wouldn't clear the breach. When all was seated, the lock was kicked loose and the primer inserted into the breech. The men jumped clear and fired. The book says you can do it in 30 seconds. The men in the *Washington* got it down to 14 seconds.

During daily trials, the Kingfisher airplanes carried on the *Washington* were catapulted off their mounts to conduct dummy torpedo drills and tracking exercises. Many days a destroyer would be sent to the horizon to serve as a target for main battery tracking drills. The chief spotter topside sent the ever changing data down to the plotting room where the main battery plotting officer ran the 100 men crew and its "computers."

The spotter's target coordinates were recalculated for each battery of guns on the 728-foot long ship. The typical firing sequence was to "bracket" the rounds — fire from the first calculations, then recalculate to the other side of the target. The spotters would relay down to the plotting room how close the second round came to the target. The third round, hopefully, would hit the target.

The British at Scapa Flow were impressed by the *Washington's* accuracy during training drills in the North Atlantic using towed targets. But the officers of the *Washington* wanted to hone that accuracy, increase their speed of firing, and drill the crew to where their actions were automatic and accurate. Mel's job at his battle station was to relay data from the plotting room up to the crew at one set of 5-inch guns. Being below deck, he never actually saw battle action.

September 13, two weeks after passing through the Panama Canal, Army patrol bombers flew in from the western horizon to form an overhead antisubmarine patrol, escorting the battleship and its destroyers into its first safe harbor of the Pacific action, Tongabatu, south of the Samoa and Fiji Islands. The *Washington* was to join Task Force (TF) 17. The battle force formed around the air carrier *Hornet*. From there they steamed west to Noumea, New Caledonia, the first large island group east of Australia.

The news at Noumea was not good. On September 14, the Marines sent reinforcements into Guadalcanal. In support against Japanese interference, the carrier *Wasp*, the battleship *North Carolina*, cruisers and destroyers were sent to the southernmost extremity of the Solomons chain. During the afternoon of September 15, Japanese submarines spotted the carrier group and put a spread of torpedoes in the *Wasp*, the *North Carolina*, and the destroyer *O'Brien*. The carrier *Wasp* was abandoned and scuttled, the *North Carolina* returned to Pearl Harbor for repairs. That left the newly arrived *Washington* as the only battleship in the Pacific alongside the *Hornet*, the only carrier.

MEB

**12 September 1942, Saturday — The South
Seas** — Tomorrow we are scheduled to put in at Tongatabu,
an island of the Tonga or Friendly group. In fact, it will be
Monday as we skip a day going over the date line. It would
happen that we'd go over on Sunday so we won't have a day
of rest evidently. Of course at sea, one day is the same as the
rest.

I've worked under more varied conditions since we left
New York than at any time since 1919 when I put the butter
ladle in the ash tray of the cook stove. These storerooms
have been extremely hot. We have to keep the doors closed
to maintain watertight integrity — just in case.

Tomorrow morning, also, will be our 21st day at sea — of
course, we stopped at Panama overnight but we were on
the water just the same. These islands we are fueling at are
SW of Samoa and Pago Pago. The last few days we have
passed the Cook, Tahiti and many other small splotches of
land that dot this immense Pacific. Of course, we didn't see
them but we know they are there. We are 1,500 miles from
the Solomon group where we'll probably be before too long.
When we arrive at Tonga we are to take on an Admiral and
then we will be the flagship of another task force — our
number this time, someone said, will be NO6. (Up North it
was Task Force 99).

To continue — It seems that this weather does things to the
sailors. The sick bay is chock full of really sick men. Some
sort of fever, cold and what not. I don't feel too well neither
but it's not that cause. Yesterday morning I tried a little
reducing exercises. Well today, I am just about done for. It's
just like I'd have run a mile or more. I think I'll just let the
bay window ride.

Again today, I fixed up my hair — this time by a barber. It
looks much better now — similar to a closely shaven wheat
field, where only shortly before tall grain stood.

As my right hand man now is in sickbay, I have had my hands busy today. I have been locating necessary spare parts that perhaps may come in handy in battle— and putting them in lockers closer to the machines down in machinery spaces No. 2 and 3.

Yesterday, while on watch we fired a few shots at a burst and Computer 3 with Mounts 5 and 7 really hit. Not to brag, but this combination is considered the most accurate on the ship. The computer crew contains Ens Melvin, W.R. Irbin, V.M. Janes, R.T. Gilmore, Madiosky, LaVine and MEB. We hope it does not turn when the Zeros come over. Good night.

14 September, Monday— When this day started out it was Sunday morning, now it's Monday night. We gained a day as quick as you can snap your finger.

Finally, after 21-1/2 days we anchored in Tongatabu. It has been a grueling three weeks at sea. Up every morning at 4:30, watches until midnite, or from midnite on. It's really a grind. I can sit down anywhere and fall asleep in five minutes anytime. Come on Beck snap out of it. This is WAR.

Tonight we are refueling— somewhere near a million gallons. We received our Admiral and are now "Task Force G." Scuttlebutt has it that we won't be long in Tabu before we toodle on. Action awaiting, sailors.

There are many numerous islands around here in this group all covered with white sand beaches and palm trees or whatever they are— maybe coconut— and headhunters. It reminds me a little of Portland, Maine. It is a British owned island and inhabited by olive colored natives. When we got in this morning the natives sailed over and sold necklaces of shells, skull bones, grass skirts and other trinkets. I never saw them but several of the fellows bought some.

The tanker that is refueling us is a civilian owned outfit run by the Merchant Marine and guns manned by U.S. sailors. They were 35 days coming from Frisco to Honolulu. Sometimes 4 knots was their speed, and unescorted all the way. That's the life I'd like, rugged and full of excitement. I have often heard people say they would like to be marooned

BECKSTRAND

W.R. Irbin

on a South Sea Island with Dot Lamour.[1] Maybe alright, but I have my doubts.

15 September, Tuesday—Excitement reigns supreme on the USS*W.* this afternoon. Less than 24 hours after we drop anchor, we are ordered to get underway again. At 4:30 p.m. Tuesday, Sept. 15 we are moving towards Tokyo. (I hope not Tokio, N.D. either.) We have received word that a force of Japanese battleships and aircraft carriers are on their way toward Tonga. In fact, the land-based scouting planes based here on Tonga Island reported ships on the horizon out at sea.

Our destroyers are already out keeping a vigil and guard until we can get underway. There was liberty for the second section and they ordered extra shore patrol and police to go over on the beach and round them up. All soldiers visiting on the ship were ordered off. I hope we engage the enemy this time.

The *North Carolina*, the *Quincy*, the *Vincennes*, and the *Chicago*. The *Vin* sunk with a reported 750 lives. The *N.C.* shot down 23 out of 25. The *Quincy* and *Chicago* were also sunk.

18 September, 1942, Friday—It is at present 2 p.m., Friday afternoon. We have just joined a large force of 12 or 15 ships here in the Coral Sea. Yesterday we passed near the Fijis and at present are east of New Hebrides looking for trouble and Japanese. No doubt both will loom over the horizon before too long a time.

It is hard to realize what a strain this is on a feller. We are at our battle stations when the sun goes down. We are there again at four in the morning. Then during the day on different occasions we gather around and prepare for action. To top it off—24 hours daily of vigilant watches. Oh well, that's what we're out here for.

The first night we left Tonga, a submarine was picked up by the detection units of the destroyers. We immediately prepared for action and speeded up our ship. The destroyer went several miles out on the horizon in search of her. The

Solomon Islands are getting closer.

What a life — ho' hum. Sleepy.

19 September, Saturday — Except for spending most of my time in plot I have nothing to report. We are heading for the Solomons where, according to official U.S. Navy communiques, a large Jap fleet is organizing for a renewed effort to recapture Guadalcanal.

As I am writing this, stations were called as a sub had been picked up — also our speed is being stepped up. The giant turbines are throbbing convulsively, the speed has been increased 6 knots so far (to 22) and still going up.

Flash! The *San Diego* has reported seeing a periscope on the starboard quarter.

Washington	BB-56	*Aaron Ward*	D-483 (sunk)
Hornet	07 (since sunk)	*Buchanan*	D-484
San Francisco	C38 (damaged)	*Farenholt*	D-491
North Hampton	C26 (sunk)	*Lardner*	D-487
Salt Lake City	C25	*Mugford*	D-389
Pensacola	C24 (severe dmg)	*Barton*	D-599
Juneau	C52 (sunk)	*Meade*	D-602
San Diego	C53	*Plunkett*	D-431

(late additions)
Atlanta (sunk)
Helena

Morris	D417	*Guadalupe*	A332
Duncan	D445	*Cimarron*	A322
Lang	D399	*Russell*	D414
Hughes	D410		

Morris, Mustin, Benham, Lansdowne, Walke[2]

21 September, 1942, Monday Morning 2:25 a.m. — Still browsing around the Coral Sea. Yesterday we were joined by another task force which makes something over 40 ships in our group. When you look out over the clear, placid Pacific waters towards the horizon, and even over the horizon, you see ships, more ships and ships' masts. And not too far out of sight is another force of 30 ships ready to unite whenever the occasion arises. We hope to annihilate the Japanese. The total of these forces represent approximately 60,000 sailors.

Yesterday the word was passed over the P.A. system of our purpose and aim as far as the present info warrants. The Japs are assembling near the Bismarck Arch. This includes the brand new super Japanese battleship. He said parts of the force that joined us yesterday had just landed reinforcements in Guadalcanal which included 5,000 troops and quantities of supplies. I understand that's the way they work things out here. Supply ships and oil tankers supply and refuel ships right here at sea.

The *North Carolina* was out at sea for 92 days. We probably will be as long. It is a month since we left New York, and stopped only twice along the way. The strain is telling on the crew already.

As you have already noted, it is a trifle early in the morning. One of the toughest physical obstacles along about this time of day is overcoming the inevitable desire to fall asleep. But when we think that no one else is looking out for us out here, and that no one else can keep awake for us, we manage to muster the necessary stamina for keeping on the ball. To bolster this we have a joepot down here, but as there are along about 100 men here in the two plotting rooms, one pot does not go far. If I had a percolator, I could make a fortune. Not a nickel a cup, but a dime or more. I know a good cup of joe[3] would have been more than welcome on more than one instance with me.

Many of my cronies know my liking for sardines—well hold on. Five of us bought a case which contains 100 cans. We also bought a case of beans, 48 cans, and a case of potted ham, 24 cans. If I was anywhere else, I would turn my back on this combination but it comes in mighty handy in the wee hours of the morning. It goes to show a feller can get along with almost anything.

The other day we had our whites dyed brown. Now one can't go on top side with whites, where it used to be, if you didn't have them they would boot you down. Dyed uniforms or dungarees are now the uniform.

Just a few minutes ago radar had a target. Stations were called, powder and ammunition was in the hoists. We were about to fire at a target which was apparently following our wake. It was identified as one of our escorts. Submarines have been sighted every day and depth changes have dropped, but one never knows whether it was sunk — especially the crew.

23 September, Wednesday morning 3:25 — Still cruising. Earlier in the night we picked up land (not visual) which was part of the New Hebrides group. It seems we have lost part of our force and what's up I don't know. (I never do for that matter.) Anyway we haven't crossed paths with the dirty Japs, which are the cause of my being up this time of the day.

23 September, Wednesday 11:10 p.m. — Our position this evening was 179.11 and 18.29. We are back near the Fiji Islands. As I said before, I don't know where we are or what the scoop is.

```
Sunrise: 0654                    USS WASHINGTON
Thursday,Sept.24,1942    "ORDERS FOR THE DAY"
Fresh Water Consumption—
Tuesday 300 gallons
NOTES:
   1. The following instructions from C-in-C
Pacific Fleet are quoted for compliance:
   "The keeping of personal diaries, journals or
records containing details of, or references to,
war-time operations is prohibited as a possible
source of information to the enemy in case of
capture or compromise."
```

29 September, Tuesday—Arrived back at Tongatubu the 26th. As you see the preceding note, my following notations will be brief. When we arrived back we received some very disheartening news. The *Wasp* was sunk, the *North Carolina* very badly damaged by torpedoes, the *South Dakota* ran aground so we are the only major new battleship in this vicinity. I hate to admit it but the Japanese are whipping our Navy very badly. It seems we can't get going.

Well, we took on a few supplies from the *Talamanca* F15. Yesterday, Monday, I was over on the island—very interesting. Came back with 75 cents more than I went over with, besides souvenirs.

While eating our noon meal yesterday, mail call went. You should have seen the cheers go up. Just like a winning touchdown or a ball game or one of Roosevelt's fireside chats. It was really amusing. Well I didn't know if I had any letters or not, and if they weren't air mail, I wouldn't have. Well, somebody must have had hunches to send them air mail, as I received 11. One of them I wished I hadn't gotten. Another friend lost, it seems, according to the letter.

Several mornings I have gone over swimming at the Queen's Isle of Patamoirita. Very swell beach, but mighty salty water.

30 September 1942, Wednesday—Today we eased over and played ball at the Navy air field. And what a ball game. I won't do any explaining here but will tell any who ask. Anyway we beat them 11-7. Pretty stiff this evening.

4 October 1942, Sunday—Well today is Sunday. We went over to the 147th Inf. Army Camp here today—Zanello and I. Very interesting, but I'll take the Navy any day.

***

Mel's journal becomes sketchy. But perhaps, there are more reasons than orders. In the daily grind of drills and training and the humid heat of the tropics, the romance of Navy duty wore off. And too, the routine earlier in the war gave Mel more time and more privacy to write. In the Pacific war zone, they were at general quarters before dawn, and often late into the night. By the time they also got their various jobs done, there was only time to sleep. And, very little of that.

October's entries are brief, somewhat cryptic. Mel's mid-November entries do no justice to the history made. So we'll turn to the collection of magazine articles and Navy histories that Mel accumulated over the years after the war to fill in the gaps left by his journal.

American forces were short in numbers — the buildup of ships and personnel was still a year away. So "scratch" forces were common — units working together on short notice with no chance to train together. Such scratch forces were the source of near calamities. And, there were many lessons to be learned in the wide expanses of the tropical seas.

Within days of the *Washington* arriving in the South Pacific, they heard from survivors of earlier battles how flammable materials made the insides of cruisers into raging hells. So, to prepare for battle, the crew was told to strip the ship of flammables, ripping up and tossing over the side the linoleum floor coverings, cans of paints, curtains.

Early in October, 2,800 men of the 164th Infantry Regiment, a national guard unit from the Dakotas, were sent to reinforce the hard pressed Marine division defending Henderson Field on Guadalcanal. The *Washington* left safe harbor at Noumea, New Caledonia, to meet up with the transports and escort them north to Guadalcanal.

Meanwhile, the Japanese continued to supply and reinforce their troops in the Solomons via nighttime runs of the Tokyo Express. Every time they left, they fired at Henderson Field. At dawn, the planes from Henderson Field bombarded any lingering Japanese ships within range. Saturday, October 10, the *Washington* learned from scouts that a Japanese cruiser force was steaming down the Slot. The *Washington*, escorting the troop-ladened transports, altered course to stay out of reach. The rest of the battle force of 13 ships headed to the western entrance of Ironbottom Sound skirting Cape d'Esperance, beating the Japanese force by only 30 minutes. The Japanese were taken by surprise, but the Battle of d'Esperance was inconclusive. The Americans lost a destroyer and another was badly damaged. The Japanese lost a destroyer and a cruiser. The Japanese were stopped from making a major bombardment of Henderson field, but the Tokyo Express made it through with its supplies.

The *Washington* and the transports with the Dakota infantry waited out the battle 250 miles away. Tuesday, October 13, the transports landed the 164th Infantry on Guadalcanal. The next day, the Japanese steamed into Ironbottom Sound and bombarded Henderson Field, and on the 15th the Tokyo Express landed 4,500 troops during the night. At dawn, a scratch force of planes from Henderson Field destroyed three of the departing transports.

Ivan Musicant wrote in his history of the *Washington*, "Like fighters able to cut and bleed their opponent, each side had meted out and received severe punishment, but neither was strong enough to deliver a killing blow. So long as the Marines and the Dakota guardsmen held Henderson Field, the key to the campaign, Japanese naval forces were denied free daytime movement. When the Japanese provided air cover for daylight runs of the Tokyo Express, they were shot down at a rate of 10 to one. Between 16 and 25 October, 103 enemy aircraft were destroyed, as compared to 14 American."[4]

MEB

16 October, Friday night—Mr. Fargo says, "We are going in to recapture Guadalcanal tomorrow morning. Everybody be on the alert. If G.Q. goes during the night, get down to your battle stations on the double. They have a large force and we are outnumbered. It being a small group of Marines at the island, we are putting all our effort in the attack."

Everyone—that is the biggest majority of the men—are all revved up for the run in. After all that is our purpose. We don't know how long we'll last, as an irritable and fatigued nature is prevalent in all hands. We go on for sheer doggedness. We cannot quit on account of the loss of sleep and good food.

18 October, Sunday, 4 a.m. — We didn't go into battle, but were instead almost caught in a trap. That would have been our doom. As we went into the night, several groups of Jap planes plotted our course — where we should be at such and such a time. They relayed this message to their ships (we intercepted it and high tailed out). Anyway, we evaded a mighty superior force — no match at all. To our one battleship, they had four new ones, in addition to cans, aircraft carrier. Now we are heading south and east again.

Oh if we only had more battleships and carriers we'd blast them Japs clear to Tokyo.

22 October, Thursday — We were chased into Esperitos Santos Island this afternoon. As there happened to be a partially loaded tanker, we immediately took on fuel. An attack was imminent, so we took out again at 8:30 p.m. The place had been shelled the night before. In the harbor was a torpedoed supply ship. What a sight. Only a few days previous 100 sailors were brought here and buried.

***

By late October, the Japanese fleet waited to the north for Henderson Field to be captured so they could retake the island. The *Washington* and its escorts were ordered into the waters south of Guadalcanal to engage any Japanese reinforcements or bomardment groups coming down the Slot. Monday, October 26, the Japanese air forces heading south and American airplanes heading north clashed head on, but continued to their respective targets. In the Battle of the Santa Cruz Islands that day, the Japanese sunk the carrier *Hornet* and a destroyer with only two of their carriers getting damaged. But, they lost 100 of their planes. The Japanese would not commit their carrier air forces again until June, 1944, in the campaign for the Marianas.

The *Washington* and its Task Force 64 spent the day of that battle steaming 150 miles south of Guadalcanal waiting to intercept a Tokyo Express that never ran that night. During the night of October 27, a torpedo was spotted and they did an emergency turn. Two hours later, another pair of torpedoes appeared, they executed another crash turn and speed increase. About 500 yards off the starboard quarter, the torpedoes "porpoised"— broke the surface and exploded in the battleship's wake.

MEB

25-26 October, Sunday, Monday—(Threw $8000 paint over side) 19 hours at battle stations. Chased Jap fleet into another task force.

27 October 0327—Two torps fired at bow, missed by yards. G.Q. 0550, three more fired, one glazed side and exploded 300 yards from ship. "A phenomenal ship thus far"—Mr. Fargo.

***

They headed back to safe harbor at Dumbea Bay, Noumea. In the next days, both sides reinforced their garrisons on Guadalcanal. Friday, October 30, two batteries of Marine field artillery landed. Two days later the Tokyo Express deposited 1,500 troops east of Henderson Field. The Japanese planned a big reinforcement for November 13-14 with 13,500 troops to be brought in with 11 transports. Destroyers would escort the transports while battleships and cruisers would bombard Henderson Field in preparation for the ground attack.

The U.S. Navy prepared all available forces, but they were still outnumbered. The *Enterprise* was the only functional carrier and the *Washington* and the *South Dakota* the only battleships. Cruisers and destroyers completed their modest forces.

Wednesday, November 11, the battle line left Dumbea Bay. Air reconnaissance on both sides tracked each other's movements. Because the slower carrier and battleships would never make it in time to thwart the Japanese bombardment group, the American ships regrouped. A scratch force of cruisers and destroyers sped ahead to intercept the Japanese.

That night, as the Japanese forces were coming down the Slot in heavy thunderstorms, the American cruiser group heading west made radar contact at 1:30 a.m. The two lines of battleships met in the night. They were so close and so interspersed, there was confusion and friendly fire. Of the 13 American ships, only five escaped heavy damage or sinking. The Japanese lost a battleship, two destroyers sunk and three others severely damaged. The Japanese gave up their plan to bombard Henderson Field that night. The opening round of the Naval Battle of Guadalcanal was over by 0200.

The night of November 13-14 the Japanese moved to conduct the bombardment and land their troops. Rear Admiral "Ching" Lee on the *Washington* left the escort of the damaged ships and headed back to Guadalcanal with his task force of two battleships and four destroyers. The Japanese bombardment group started shelling Henderson Field. The Tokyo Express began moving in down the Slot and shortly after dawn were halfway down the slot when Henderson Field scouts spotted them. Six of the transports were sunk in the pounding given by planes from Henderson Field, the carrier *Enterprise*, and bombers stationed at Espiritu Santo.

During the daytime air battle Rear Admiral Lee stayed on his flagship *Washington* 100 miles to the southwest. He figured the Japanese forces would be back that night. As they approached Guadalcanal in the early night hours, a U.S. PT squadron came upon them. Not knowing who they were, the sailors on the little PTs broadcast their positions clearly. Musicant reports that "Ching" Lee, knowing the danger, transmitted a plain language message that would enter history (probably inaccurately) as "Damn the torpedoes, full speed ahead."[5]

15-16 November, Sunday, Monday—Battle Royal
Left out November 11, Returned November 17

***

The naval battle of November 15 would be chronicled many times in detail after the war. That night, the Japanese battleship *Kirishima*, two heavy cruisers and nine destroyers planned to do the bomardment of Henderson airfield that wasn't accomplished the previous nights. Lee's task force was a scratch group and poorly balanced—the destroyers chosen because of their remaining fuel supply.

It was a calm, warm night. The ships sailed in total blackout and quiet by the light of a quarter moon. At 11 p.m., the *Washington's* radar picked up the Japanese ships. They fired fore and aft, and the Japanese made a smoke screen and reversed. Soon, the rest of TF64 met up with the rest of the Japanese ships. Within 10 minutes, TF 64's destroyers were out of the fight. *Walke, Preston, Benham, Gwin*—two were sunk, two badly damaged. The Japanese lost one ship in the initial rounds.

The two battleships in the task force steamed on, the *Washington* ahead of the *South Dakota*. The *South Dakota* had taken some hits that shorted out its electrical power. The *Washington* turned to keep the burning and sinking ships between her and the enemy, to avoid having the battleship silhouetted in the fires and visible in the night sky.

The *South Dakota*, with no communication abilities, didn't follow the *Washington*. The crew of the *Washington* didn't know that since their radar had a blind spot to the rear. As soon as the *South Dakota* was silhouetted by the burning ships, the Japanese switched on their spotlights. The *Washington* crews fired and put out the lights. The second Japanese ship flipped on its spotlights, the same response from the *Washington*. The third ship picked up the *South Dakota* in its spotlights and the *South Dakota* started taking hits. By now the *South Dakota* partially restored her electrical power and began firing, though she still didn't communicate with the *Washington*.

The Japanese battleship, *Kirishima* had been picked up moments before on radar by the *Washington*, but it withheld fire being uncertain exactly where the *South Dakota* was. When the *Kirishima* trained its spotlights on the *South Dakota*, it identified her and started firing at a point-blank range of 8,400 yards. At exactly midnight, the *Washington's* first salvo of 16-inch shells straddled the Japanese battleship. The second salvo hit on the superstructure and 30 seconds later the third salvo landed directly square.

Hidden in the dark behind the burning ships, the *Washington* had surprised the Japanese. It fired 75 16-inch shells, scoring nine direct hits, plus 40 more with the 5-inch batteries. The *Kirishima* was in flames, listing and steaming in circles. It was scuttled and sunk by its fellow ships later that morning. At 12:33, with the Japanese battleship out of action, Admiral Lee turned to draw the Japanese destroyers and cruisers away from the *South Dakota*. As it turned, torpedoes were spotted and for the next 45 minutes it zigzagged to dodge 17 torpedo attacks before the Japanese gave up the chase. The *Washington* had taken only one 5-inch hit.

The Japanese plans for bombardment were stopped, but not the transports—four with 2,000 Japanese troops started unloading. At dawn, the planes from Henderson Field and the carrier *Enterprise* attacked. The men and supplies made it ashore, but it was to be the last attempt by the Japanese to wage offensive war.

Hard fighting still lay ahead for the American Marines, Army soldiers and guardsmen on Guadalcanal. Despite its setback, the Tokyo Express still ran. But the turning point of the war had been reached. No comparable Japanese effort was mounted to interfere with the operations from Henderson Field, or with the reinforcement of American troops who would soon force the enemy to abandon Guadalcanal, and skillfully withdraw.

In port at Noumea after the battle, Rear Admiral Lee vacated his sea cabin just aft of the bridge and offered it as the ship's new radar room. The Battle of Guadalcanal had shown the blind spot to their rear might be fatal—they nearly waited too long not knowing the *South Dakota* had not followed behind them. The *Washington's* crew put up a sheet of plexiglass between the radar room and the bridge where both sides could see the plotting. It was an innovation to be adopted by the entire Navy before the war was over.

Left out of Noumea **December 7, Monday morning**. A cloudy, rainy and dreary day.

***

One year after the bombing of Pearl Harbor, Mel Beckstrand had experienced war, and had little to say.

As December and January wore on, the Japanese continued to try to provision their troops on Guadalcanal. Submarines could only deliver two days supplies, so they resorted to floating metal drums crammed with goods into shore. The Japanese Navy finally convinced their Army to evacuate Guadalcanal and retreat to the island New Georgia in the central Solomons. It was a retreat of less than 200 miles, but it was a strategic retreat that would continue in the months ahead.

January 4 and 5, the *Washington* and TF 64 provided heavy support for landing more troops on Guadalcanal. They thought the Japanese were going to try to retake Guadalcanal, so they planned an operation to lure the Japanese into a battle in waters south of Guadalcanal. The Japanese were planning to evacuate, and refused the bait. They landed some backup troops, and in the ensuing battle of Rennel Island sunk another US Navy cruiser.

At the end of January, the *Washington* and TF64 were heading back to the Solomons, practicing night drills as they steamed north. The night of February 3, the Japanese began the first of three night operations to evacuate their Guadalcanal garrison, taking off almost 12,000 troops. On February 8, U.S. Army forces completed the conquest of Guadalcanal and the nearby island of Tassafaronga. The islands passed into American hands exactly six months after the first Marines waded ashore.

The U.S. war effort at home was beginning to pick up momentum. New ships and new reinforcements were arriving steadily. Several experienced men from the *Washington* were transferred to the arriving ships. And, in turn, Mel Beckstrand found himself in a new battle station—out of the air conditioned plotting room and up to the handling room for Number Three 5-inch mount. For once he could see what was happening, and he had a bit more privacy to write in his notebook. After two months with no entries—and four months since a lengthy entry—Mel started journaling again.

February 43

Here it is Tuesday morning, February 2, 1943. A year ago we had just arrived in Philadelphia. Where will we be on Groundhog Day of 1944? The day—overcast, sultry, with an occasional wisp of wind which is truly refreshing.

The weather I would say is a bit squally, sort of the Scapa Flowian type. At the very moment the sun is beating down heartily and a beautiful rainbow is visible.

As this is being penned—or penciled I should say—I am sitting on a little 'skow' up here on the boat deck (the deck clock just tolled four gongs which is 1000). We are to fuel in a few minutes. A few thousand yards out the *Indiana* is just winding up operations. It will be the first time I have seen a battleship fuel at sea. Yesterday we pumped fuel into three "cans".

The reason for our fueling out here—approximately 400 miles southwest of Guada—is perhaps we may have to intercept the Bougainville Express[6] which contains, this time, 25 warships—16 cans, the remainder cruisers and battleships. Originally we had planned on going in tomorrow.

The Pacific today is a trifle rough—really smooth, though, compared with the typhoon of the last few days. When the water isn't rough from wind, the ground swells cause quite a disturbance. On several occasions fueling cans, they have lurched into the side of our ship, causing us minute damage but jarring the DD's considerably. One time in particular, the destroyer sprung a leak and its wake was like a horizontal rainbow.

All about me and below me, sailors are rushing to and fro to have everything in readiness. No time can be wasted as we are vulnerable to torpedoes—you see, our speed is cut down to about 8 or 9 knots. While one ship is fueling, the others keep a vigilant eye for bobbing periscopes. We are about to catapult another plane also for reconnaissance purposes. As I was mentioning the crew preparing for fueling, bo'suns readying lines for the purpose of lashing the two ships together. The oil kings have already bolted on the rubber hosing that transfers the oil. Electricians to my left are untangling a long lead for a phone to communicate between ships. The jobs are not too large but highly important—cooperation is essential. Well, the plane is still

purring away. Soon they will train the catapult out and fire
her away—Bang! There she goes with a roar like Kelly's
truck. A fine getaway for being heavily loaded—two depth
charges (600 lbs.) and full capacity gasoline. The plane is the
Kingfisher type, one wing, monoplane.

1205—I have just finished noonday chow (no beans).
Now I am on watch in the upper handling room of Mount III.
Last time we were in Noumea several men were transferred.
One (my sidekick) left, and also left a vacancy in the watch
bill. What a letdown after being in the air-conditioned spaces
of the plotting room for over a year. The heat is terrific.
Perspiration runs little rivulets down the ravines of one's
frame. I just swam over to another part of the space. If I
had my fishing rod, I could cast in the pool being formed
at my elbows—I always wanted to do a little salt water
fishing. My nostrils cringe at the vexatious odors of eight
shiny bodies and 16 calloused, toe-jammed feet. Oh, there
is a ventilation tube coming down from the mount but some
shower-detesting sailor sits prominently at the opening, and
it wouldn't surprise me if somebody's buttocks were propped
against its upper entrance to cool his bean-scorched cheeks.
It's a fact, me lady. I squirm as 100 gremlins pierce the hills
and valleys of the plains of abdomen. Oh—aforementioned
phrase is for the rash I have contracted on the panes of my
bay window.

I find it amusing, but not very conducive to morale, to
think of the wedding I would like to have someday. This idea
of being out here month after month without the breath of a
fragrantly scented girl near you—the enticing feeling of her
hands running through the once profuse locks of hair—sets
a feller's mind awandering. Will it ever happen again?

Anyway, we were going to a wedding. At this gala soiree,
I would want it strictly feminine. Girls to the right of me, to
the left of me. Women in the pews, girls in the choir, and of
course, it would have to be one by my side or it wouldn't be
legal. The best man must be a woman, flower girls galore.
The ushers could be more on the portly side, but still women

you understand. The person issuing the oath has not been designated.

3 February, Wednesday 2:30 p.m. — On the placid looking waters of the Coral Sea below San Cristobol and Santa Cruz we have spent most of the day looking for Nips. The word has been passed that a Zero has been downed by one of our scouting planes operating from the *Sarotoga* of this task force. We have a force of 17 ships — three BB's, one carrier, one cruiser and 12 DD's. Our formation goes thusly —

	DD	DD	DD	DD	
	San Juan		*North*		
DD	AA Cruiser		*Carolina*		DD
		Carrier			
DD		*Saratoga*			DD
	Indiana		*Washington*		
	DD	DD	DD	DD	

You can see what the Japs gun for is the carrier. In this formation however they would have to fly through plenty of steel to reach it.

5 February, Friday, 1630 — Flash — A second plane has been shot down within 10 miles of our then position.

Yesterday (Thursday the fourth) we shot down a Nippo bomber. While on the main deck during the afternoon, I chanced to see a portion of the wreckage of the Mitsu 99 float by. Later in the day, one of our destroyers picked up the seven crew members — one was "hari-carried"[7] when being rescued. The remaining six were taken to Espiritu Santo by the Jenkins. For some time we believed they were coming on board the *Washington*.

Operating out here in the Coral area is Admiral Giffin who was with us in Iceland and Scapa Flow. He is a rugged individual, both in speech and stature. The Admiral we have on here now is Vice Admiral Lee, a frail looking fellow, but possessing an adequate repartee.

We have received several messages from Giff during the past few days. "Send me air coverage" was one message.

The curt reply of Lee followed "What in the #&! do you mean, aren't the Japs covering you?"

On another occasion Lee radioed Giffin, "Better take it easy out here Giffin. The Japs use a little different techniques than the Germans."

This time Giffin retorted, "The San Francisco went within 6,000 yards of those yellow #&!* — I'll board their ship." That's just the way that fellow is.

On our last convoy to Murmansk in July we were about to contact the *Von Tirpitz*. Had it not been for the superiority of the Limey Admiral's rank perhaps we would have been chipping ice in Davy Jones' ice box now. The German plan at that time was to suck us into flying distance of the Norwegian coast where the Jerries' had numerous land-based planes. I have since then appreciated the judgment of the Commander of the Home Fleet, but you can't help but respect the Giffin style.

Well to get things squared away, Lee said he would order air and surface coverage from Guadalcanal. They came out with ONE destroyer and ONE plane. I imagine the old Giffin is fuming these days on the wonderful response.

But he also has his good points. Once when the fleet was coming in from maneuvers into Scapa he sighted some Scotsmen fishing ahead. Rather than break their nets he ordered the entire fleet turned to starboard thus saving the Scotsman's cod (and next winter's cud). (Pretty punk Beck.)

8 February Monday — We were this morning in the middle of the Coral Sea heading west and northwest at 21 knots. All through the night we have been hitting this speed. I think it is an all out battle soon to finish what has been going on for the past several days. Today we'll meet the remaining ships of Admiral Giffin's force. In the press this morning, Secretary Knox mentioned a major clash as a finale for the present great battle.

At present, I am on watch in Upper Mount 3. I am sitting on some powder casks, and from a small porthole, I can see the crew preparing for battle. The word has been passed for all hands to put bedding in fireproof bags. A clean sweep down was ordered to clean litter and trash from all decks, eliminating fire hazards. Showers are recommended and clean clothing put on. Usually lights are out in the afternoon, so men can catch up on much needed sleep. This afternoon all lights are on and an unusual amount of activity prevalent. When we go to battle stations, I'll give a blow by blow description, providing of course, we contact the Nips. I hope we do—they'll wish they'd have stayed home and grown rice.

The time is now 8:15 P.M. Monday the 8th. We are at our battle stations anticipating any eventuality which Tojo has to offer. Before the call to stations was sounded this evening, we were lounging around on topside taking in a few breaths of exhilarating South Sea air. In the distance, we could count a total of 35 warships—24 destroyers, six cruisers, two carriers (*Saratoga* and *Enterprise*) and three battleships (*Indiana, North Carolina* and *Washington*) and we were told that additional forces were at our disposal. It is a potent looking fleet indeed, ready for action. It involves an aggregate of some 30,000 sailors.

We were also told this afternoon that on February 11 the Japanese are celebrating their 2,000th anniversary of military supremacy. Somehow or other, I feel it will stop at such. We'll try our best to let their record ride at a round figure.

12 February Friday—After 17 days at sea we are home again—at least we must call it home (Noumea). Anyway, we will have mail, I hope. That is, if my friends haven't forsaken me.

With approximately 100 rounds of firing, we wound up the Guadalcanal campaign. It has been a long hard grind (six months). In its occupation many lives have been lost, many ships sunk. Those involved would be grateful, indeed, for a two week leave from the theaters of this war-beleaguered section. Shave off the beard that has dressed our faces through numerous battles, wipe the haggard look from our eyes, and really enjoy life. That day will be welcome indeed.

But for now, abandon this wistful thinking. With just enough time for refueling, and a few meager supplies taken on we are underway again. This morning we were 660 miles west of Noumea (21 February, Sunday). Quartermaster Shay told us since the commissioning of the ship she had traveled 101,000 nautical miles — or more than four times around the globe. No grass growing under our feet, I would say.

***

The *Washington* left Dumbea Bay with TF64 on February 19 to support the occupation of the Russell Islands. For the *Washington* and TF64 this was the end of their active participation in the Solomons. In the Bismarck Sea, 1,600 miles to the northwest, the U.S. Army and Australian air forces hailed a great victory in the first days of March. The Japanese had decided to reinforce their garrison north of New Guinea in the Admiralty Islands. They were spotted by an army airplane and within two days, all eight transports and three destroyers were sunk. It was the last time the Japanese ventured convoys into waters dominated by Allied air power.

Life on the *Washington* continued in the daily grind. On March 10, the *Washington* led the task force, now four battleships strong, out for exercises. The gunnery drills included firing at towed sleeves pulled at the end of cables by the Kingfishers. The daily weather balloon released to gather atmospheric pressure and wind direction were used for target practice once their data collecting duties were finished. Night maneuvers were practiced.

11 March, Thursday — We are at sea again. This time we have the *Massachusetts* with us. That gives us four new battleships. I think we are out for gunnery. In fact, we have done considerable shooting already.

ST. PATRICK'S DAY—Yes sir, it's Pat's Day. The same as the rest however— except that we are having a typhoon. And brother, it's really blowing. It's a terrible night. Rain is pelting down like hailstones on a tin roof. The torpedo nets we have lashed along our sides are banging with a terrific din. All day preparations have been made for an expected 85 mile gale by midnight. Special sea detail has been stationed. The officer of the deck has shifted his watch to the bridge, everything in readiness to get underway in case the powers of wind and wave tear us from our moorings. Great would be the catastrophe for the "Mighty *W*" to be dashed among the rocks.

Tonight over the entire harbor of Noumea, lights are on fore and aft of every ship, merchantmen and men-of-warsmen alike. As I am sitting here in the supply office the ship seems to be trembling with increasing uneasiness. Just before I started these lines, I returned from topside of an observation. The wind was whistling through the signal cables—the mooring cables are tugging and straining at their lashings. The rain is coming down in unabated fury. Even our daily ship's recreation party over to Shangra-La was cancelled this afternoon. The last boat for the beach left early this afternoon.

Aside from the storms we had a little humor today. This morning before turn-to Usrey and I typed up a list of good IRISHMEN who would have holiday routine for the day—names like Glaviana, Yesinkevich, Levine, Kryazweski, Zanello and Thibedeau graced the list. Webb remarked that it looked like the football roster at Notre Dame—and incidentally everyone knows how Irish Notre Dame is!

Just a year ago today, 5 April, Monday we entered Scapa Flow. It has been a hectic year. We have traveled over many a stormy wave. Right now the sea is not calm. This morning we got underway. Yesterday, Sunday, we worked all day.

Sunday has no meaning anymore. Everything but, happens on that day. Gone are the serene, quiet afternoons I used to know. Oh well, this is war.

For some reason or another, we returned to Noumea on Tuesday noon. There was a gale at sea, and a good number of sailors were sick but I don't think that was the reason—unless the skipper was ill. I believe our main reason for going out was to calibrate the guns and fire a few rounds which we did.

Well this evening Zink, Webb, Usrey and myself went over on the beach after some stores. There is nothing out of the ordinary in this trip except for one thing, which I shall now relate.

Upon tying up to the dock at Noumea about 6:30 p.m. (which was of course after dark), we disembarked on a large loaded barge which, too, was tied to the dock. The barge, being heavily loaded, was well below the level of the dock. There being no gangway we had to rely upon our athletic ability to gain footing on terra-firma. Well, the sea goer (Usrey), the tall gangly Texan, reached the higher level first. Wanting to be benevolent, or plainly just showing the rest of us up, he started offering his hand in aid to the rest of us. In this manner, Webb gained safety.

My turn up. Our hands are clasped, the proceedings have started. At this stage, I find I do not have a too strong grip so I yells, "Wait a minute." Well as I said, we had already started. He quickly obeys the order, much to my chagrin, and into the drink I go. (Ordinarily this fellow is pretty reluctant on obeying orders. But seeing this opportunity he seized it—and who wouldn't. Even I wouldn't drop a shipmate over willfully—not much).

Well as I said earlier, the wind was high and to avoid the salty spray over the gunwales, I wore a raincoat. In my diving operations, I find it not too convenient. Anyway I was in the water gurgling, gargling, puffing and swimming. From what I hear, I created quite a splash. You see when I went down, the old raincoat came up —when I came up, the raincoat covered my head so I couldn't see. Not being able to see, and with a mouthful of water, I kept churning the water thinking I was still submerged. Somehow or other I cleared my vision. There I was, 100 eyes looking down gleefully (and I may say in passing—most of them were soldiers—embarrassing?? Not at all). I couldn't stay there. I looked the situation over, and swimming, of course. Not a line or chance to get out in sight. Well, just about ready to "abandon ship" I saw two black, calloused hands reaching over the side. These natives were taking it seriously—while my buddies made merry. I'll admit it must have looked funny. And it will be <u>some</u> time before I hear the last of it.

Tonight, 7 April, Wednesday we are again at sea. Something is in the offing, and I hope we are involved. Anything to break monotony. Tonight a plane cracked up on the *Saratoga*. It is still windy at gale proportions.

10 April, Saturday—At sea. This morning at 10 a.m. the word was passed over the loudspeaker "The smoking lamp is out, knock off all games, keep silence about the deck, during burial of the dead." The word "war" was brought home more than ever. The atmosphere around the ship this afternoon has a definite weirdness about it. Everything seems so different. I, myself, am so weak. I am reluctant to walk around—just a few hours ago my partner went over to sick bay to give a transfusion. That's the way it is out here in the Coral Sea south of Guadalcanal.

11 April, Sunday—Another burial at sea.

19 April, Monday—After 10 days of sea we are in port again. Immediately upon entering we provisioned, fueled, etc. All through one night we worked. Even all day Palm Sunday, and yesterday, which was Sunday, I really mashed one of my fingers. Well today is the 19th. I am 24 years too old. Seems just a few years ago I turned 16. Oh well, time just marches on.

***

On the same day that Mel hit the drink, some shipmates hit the other kind of drink. Unfortunately, they hit a batch of bad liquor. The burials at sea for the two who died were strange days for Mel, and for the other sailors who experienced their first such burial. The sailcloth wrapped body was brought on deck, laid on a mess table and covered with a flag. With a 5-inch shell of antiaircraft ammo weighing the bag at the foot of the sailor, the table was tipped and the body sent over the side. The latitude and longitude were noted in the ship's log, and given to the family with the death notice.

But that melancholy event was followed by good news. They were heading to Pearl Harbor, Territory of Hawaii (PHTH) for refitting, repairs and supplies.

30 April, Friday—Today we pulled the hook out of the murky dark waters of Noumea Harbor and took out to sea. We hope and pray we eventually end up in the States—but the popular, or should I say unpopular, current rumor is only Pearl Harbor. Tonight we are pushing on up to the Hebrides where we are scheduled to fuel, and unload any excessive stores. We expect to reach there tomorrow. Tonight the sea is unusually rough, caused mainly by ground swells. This, by the way, is our first trip out under our new skipper, J.E. Maher, formerly of the *San Juan*, an antiaircraft cruiser.

1 May, Saturday—Havannah Harbor, Efate Island, New Hebrides. Today was a busy day at this base. We arrived about noon and shoved off approximately 5:30. We are now heading east—destination unknown—but almost positively P.H.T.H., as we have passengers on here for that Island. Also some for Uncle Sugar.

In this harbor of Havannah we found more ships than we expected. The Uncle has them all over I guess. Anyway, tied up in this beautiful south sea island were the battleships *Colorado* and *Maryland*, cruisers—*Montpelier, Columbia,*

Denver and *Cleveland*, and the usual amount of cans and merchantmen.

We're still hoping for the States, and we're hoping you're hoping with us. Day by day positions from Noumea to Honolulu. All readings daily 0500

Friday, April 30	Noumea
Saturday, May 1	168° E. Long 18° S. Lat.
Sunday, May 2	170° E. Long. 16.14° Lat.
Monday & Sunday, 3 & 2	177.18° E. Long — 13.30° S. Lat.
Monday, May 3	176.33 W. Long — 9.03 S. Lat.
Tuesday, May 4	171.43 W Long. — 9.30 S. Lat.
Wednesday, May 5	167.41 W. Long. — 00.00 Lat.

One of these days is going to be the happiest or unhappiest for the crew of the Rusty "*W*". Reason: when and if this ship dry docks at Pearl Harbor. If they can handle the repairs we need, it is a certainty we won't hit the States before another year has passed.

4 May, Tuesday — When we crossed the 180th meridian, and later, the international date line, things really began to happen; first it was Sunday, then it was Monday. Then just like that it was Sunday again, and before you could get squared away, it was Monday again. Well finally, Tuesday got here and I hope before long, things will be routine again.

Today we fueled two cans: the USS *Landmer* DD 487 and USS *Russell* DD414. We will fuel two more on the morrow.

As yet I haven't mentioned the Japanese prisoner of war we have on here. If I got the treatment he gets, I wouldn't mind becoming a prisoner. He don't have to do a thing — he even has a Marine to hold his hand when he goes to the "head"[8].

Our new skipper, J.E. Maher is quite the lad. He really believes in watching the speed dial go up and down. Well, he was steaming along at 18 or 20 knots and all of a sudden he'll kick her up to 27. Quite the guy. Usually when coming out of harbors like Noumea or Havannah, Captain Davis cruised along at a speed of 12 knots. Mahers pulls the throttle down to 18 and fairly glides out. But woe betide him, and us too, if we chanced on a reef. It would tear the ship in half. Of course, coming from a highly maneuverable ship like the *San Juan*, I can readily see that he has "cruiser tactics".

For transfer to Pearl Harbor we have on here about 100 men. With us now is the *Enterprise*, a carrier of the *Yorktown* Class. She is on her way to the States after a tour of duty of nearly 30 months. I hope such luck stays clear of the *Washington*.

This morning we were 700 miles from Wahoo. We are expected to wrap the hook sometime Saturday—but I hope not for long. I'd rather see the waters of Puget Sound or San Francisco Bay grace the lines of our bow.

5 May, Wednesday—This morning we were 1,335 miles from Hawaii. From the carrier today a plane crashed on takeoff. Neither plane nor pilots were recovered. Just ordinary everyday life on a carrier. But we too have periods of excitement. Today while fueling a seaman called Reid fell into the churning waters between our ship and the can. When last seen he was waving and smiling broadly.

Tonight we are going on a speed run for 12 hours. I hope at the end they find the weakened machinery that will warrant a trip to Bremerton.

Two months later
1 August, Sunday—Well, we completed that speed run successfully, had an overhaul at Pearl Harbor and are at the present time within 30 miles of Samoa on our way south ? again.

We arrived in Pearl Harbor May 9. While there, many things happened—pleasant and otherwise. Several of our men were killed in the dry-dock—a couple more crippled badly. One was all fouled up in an auto crash.

On the other hand it was good to see civilization again. And another thing, fresh milk to drink, and believe me, I drank it, too. In the city of Honolulu we saw many things of interest. We went through Dole's pineapple factory, lounged at the Royal Hawaiian Hotel, swam in Waikiki, and even tried a hand at surf riding, toured the island, fought fires, and worked like a slave (at times).

While in for repairs, we installed 15 quads of 40MM and boy, how they can shoot. We were out on a trial run for a few days and shot down a radio controlled plane. After seeing this, I am a little leery about being a pilot. All told, we were on three trial runs. Then we got underway on July 27 — 5:00 p.m.

With us are two transports, *Mount Vernon* and *Luriline*, heavily laden with troops — 18,000. Also two tin cans. We crossed the equator at 162° west longitude on July 30 with appropriate ceremonies, and I do mean APPROPRIATE.

In Oahu one sees plenty of girls, but then, too, there are plenty of males to compete with — about 275 to 1 is the present ratio. So you see, one has to be a pretty good fellow to make out. As you have already guessed — this kid didn't make out.

I guess this is as close as we will get to the good old States for another year.

In the Navy yard one can still see the havoc wrought by those yellow #&!* in 1941. The *Oklahoma* is slowly being righted, but a close observation shows a good job of bombing was done. The *Arizona* is still almost invisible, as is the *Utah*.

One thing I've always wanted to do I did while I attended fire fighting school — put on and go down in a diving suit. And I'll truthfully say, I'll never make a diver or a sub sailor. Oh yes, Luehring and I went through a sub — HADDOCK. Very interesting, but I'll take the Rusty *"W"*. We now have a new Executive A.A. Ageton, fresh from the academy. We have already felt his strict discipline, but then a few Jap bullets past his ears up there on the bridge will ease him off.

***

The tide of the war may have turned at the Battle of Guadalcanal but it wasn't until nearly a year later in the fall of 1943, that the allied forces' real offensive began—two years after the start of the war. The immense building program bore fruit and scores of new ships had joined the fleet. The lessons learned in the early days had been studied and turned into new tactics which fitted the expanse of ocean. There were new carriers loaded down with the latest planes, new destroyers, new cruisers. They were off to push the Japanese back through their island holdings all the way to Tokyo.

MEB

Task Forces 37-38-39, **Sept 1, 1943,** on the way to Guadalcanal

Battleships	*Washington*	56	
	North Carolina	55	
	Massachusetts	59	flagship
	Maryland	46	
	Colorado	45	
Carriers	*Saratoga*	3	
	Breton		
Cruisers	*Cleveland*	55	
(light)	*Montpelier*	57	
	Denver	58	
	Columbia	56	
	San Juan	54	
	San Diego	53	

Converse	509	*Sterett*	407
Anthony	515	*Fanning*	385
Selfridge	357	*Dunlap*	384
Wilson	408	*Bennett*	473
Charles Ausburn	570	*Foote*	511
Spences	512	*Lansdowne*	486
Ralph Talbot	390	*Guest*	473
Grayson	435	*Thatcher*	514
Woodworth	460	*Patterson*	392

Stack	406	*Dyson*	572
McCalla	488	*Lardner*	487
Stanly	478	*McCall*	400
Claxton	571	*Lang*	399
Farenholt	491	*Buchanan*	484
Fullam	474		

The foregoing list of ships comprise task forces 37-38-39, of which we are a part of 38. We are now operating above Guadalcanal. We got underway August 30. This list includes over 40 ships aggregating 327,700 tons of ships. Personnel attached include over 30,000.

5 September, Sunday — Today we anchored again in Havannah Harbor after an uneventful trip at sea. Probably, we would have stayed out longer but the tanker from which we were to fuel was torpedoed and sunk. The *North Carolina* got underway today for Bremerton? or at the least, P.H.T.H. That makes about the third time she has been there, while we have been there once. For these voyages, she has been appropriately dubbed USS USO. Oh well, someone has to stay out here and keep the wolf from the door.

Effective the first of this month, I made first class. Now I'm drawing 136.80 per. We have received some mail, but not as much as I expected. Wish you people would write. This island of Efate is pretty #&!* desolate even if it is pretty. Since we've left P.H., I haven't seen a human with skirts (that is a female) and probably won't for another year. Boy, that is one thing that gets a feller down. In Pearl you could at least look at them. Oh well, now with Italy under control, maybe it won't be too long.

$$***$$

The Gilbert Islands, northeast of the Solomons were the first step in the effort to push the Japanese back in the central Pacific theater. The atolls of the Gilberts were heavily fortified by the Japanese. The plan was to have air forces hammer the Japanese air bases and fortifications while the Marines would be landed to take on the ground forces.

By November 15 the Pacific Task Forces gathered with six carriers, making cruising formations of three carriers in the center surrounded by three battleships which in turn were circled by six destroyers. One group headed to launch air strikes. The *Washington* and the other group slipped during the night into the body of water between the Gilberts and the Marshalls — between the atolls and enemy's supporting bases on the Marshall Islands. The carriers' planes bombarded the Japanese airfields on the Gilberts, and sunk the light naval forces. They waited for a response but the Japanese fleet stayed at anchor, although their submarines harassed the allied fleet. The real attack came from the Japanese torpedo bombers, which kept up the air assault until the islands were captured and the American Navy could withdraw.

Once the Gilberts were secure, the battle line was requested to smash the Japanese installations on the island of Nauru, 400 miles to the west. Many of the planes that had been attacking the fleet in the previous weeks were assumed to based or staging through Nauru, and it had to be dealt with before the upcoming invasion of the Marshall Islands. Additionally, Nauru was a major source of phosphate fertilizer for Japanese agriculture. The *Washington's* primary target was the main phosphate loading facility. The other battleships had the mission of using their 16-in guns to destroy barracks and gun placements. The 5-inch guns would take care of landing strips and hangars. At 7 a.m., December 8 they began firing. In an hour, 810 16-inch rounds pounded Nauru.

7 December 43, Tuesday — Boy we're ticking off knots for Nauru. We are on our way to give the boys up there a little reveille in the morning. That is them "Nip boys". It will be a nine gun salvo from each battlewagon — 54 in all. About 60 tons of steel bursting near your sack can't be considered pleasant to wake up with. Nauru is located 52 miles south of the equator almost due west of the Gilberts.

We have been out here since November 11, and it is

questionable when we'll get in—maybe not even for
Christmas. Chow is getting limited. We fuel at sea, and have
air raids almost at every sunset. Boy, it's really getting me
down.

8 December, Wednesday—Last time I saw Nauru—I
mean where Nauru was—it was a smoking inferno. Dense
clouds of black smoke rolled skyward. This morning we
sailed in from the north: six battleships, 12 tin cans with the
carriers out on the horizon. 7:00 a.m. was zero time. Shortly
before this, however, the planes from the *Bunker Hill* and
the *Monterrey* bombed the place. At 0700 we opened up and
continued with the 16-inch and 5-inch for 43 minutes. Over
500 tons of steel were discharged in this time.

While the planes received antiaircraft fire, not a shot was
fired at us. This shows how coy those Japs are. If they had
opened fire, we could have spotted their gun emplacement
positions and wiped them out. Thinking we had destroyed
all life, we sent a destroyer in to rescue the crew of a
plane which had been shot down. When the *Boyd* was
within range, she received a tremendous burst of fire—27
casualties were reported. Pretty shifty those Nips.

Right now, we are on our way into Havannah Harbor
in Efate. Expect to arrive the 12th. It will make us 31
continuous days at sea. All I hope when we get there, is that
there is plenty of mail.

***

Elsewhere in the Pacific, the Seventh fleet and General MacArthur's
forces were leapfrogging up the Solomons-Bismarck island chains and
along New Guinea's north coast. The Japanese base at Kavieng was a
problem. It was beyond the range of allied land based planes. The carriers
were sent to strike at Kavieng at dawn, Christmas Day. The *Washington*
spent the day north around the Solomons screening the carriers. They hit
Kavieng again on January 5.

Conquest of the Marshall Islands, the heart of the Japanese outer
defense perimeter, came swiftly, less than two months after the Gilberts

campaign. Japan had governed the 800 mile long island chain since 1920. Kwajalein Atoll, the world's largest atoll, served as the military and administrative headquarters. It lay in the center of the chain, covered by five air bases on islands around Kwajalein. The American plan was to attack Kwajalein with everything they had at the end of January.

The American forces were up to 12 carriers, three battleships, nine cruisers and 39 destroyers. January 29, the carrier planes found the Japanese base nearly empty of planes. The next day, the bombardment group, including the *Washington* moved in. The Kingfishers were catapulted off to call the fall of shot, and firing started at 8:30 a.m. In the rainy tropical day, the bombardment group threw its ammo at the coast defense guns, blockhouses, beach gun emplacements, seaplane and storage facilities. Three hours latter, they moved to the western tip of Kwajalein Island to bombard the beaches where the two regimental combat teams from the 7th Infantry Division would land the next morning.

MEB

January 30, 1944, 0945 a.m.
Room 204, Phone 563
This is the Captain to the officers and men of the
Washington.
Good shooting. Put all the bullets on the targets. This six gun salvo from three battleships is reveille for the Nips. Hit beautifully. Columns of smoke are rising. Stand by for the main battery to open fire on Berlin.

***

The next night after the bombardment of Kwajalein, February 1, was a moonless night. At 0400 the watch changed. The ship's radar helped track ships in the formation, unless they were too close, when the radar would just show "grass."

The battleship *Indiana* was spotted dead ahead. It took just 90 seconds from sighting to impact, by which time the *Washington* was slowing and beginning to turn. The call went over the speakers—"Standby for collision starboard."

90,000 tons of steel collided.

The *Washington's* bow was smashed in from the keel, 60 feet back. Within two hours, they had pumped dry all the space behind the collision, welded the holes in the bulkhead and reinforced weak areas. They headed to Majuro Atoll for emergency repairs and then on to Hawaii for fitting of a temporary bow.

March 6, they headed out of Pearl Harbor, and, when the destination, Bremerton, Wash., was announced the crew went nuts. They were headed back home. With the exception of the three day leave in New York, they had been in action for 20 months.

March 12 they arrived at Bremerton, off loaded ammunition and moved to dry dock. Waiting there was a new bow. Round the clock work had the new bow welded in place and the *Washington* ready for floating out on April 9. Within a month, it was back in the Pacific.

Mel was not to be with them. He headed home to North Dakota for a month's leave. When he returned, he along with a large number of men were reassigned to new ships. He received a promotion to Chief Petty Officer and assignment to the brand new light carrier, *Kwajalein*. Mel would continue to journal as he finished out the war on the carrier which ferried planes in the Pacific.

The allied forces in the Pacific were on a roll. General MacArthur's troops continued their advance along the New Guinea coast. By fall, November, 1944, they were in position to invade the south Philippine island of Mindanao.

For the Navy, the next stop on the central Pacific drive in June, 1944, was the Marianas — 1,000 miles ahead of the most advanced base, and fortress of the inner defense line for Japan. The *Washington* was again the flagship for Admiral Lee. They supported the air strikes pummeling enemy defenses in the Marianas on the islands of Saipan, Tinian, Guam, Rota and Paga. These were hilly islands of some size, heavily defended and well protected by air bases. The mission was for the Navy ships to absorb the sea and air attacks of the enemy, and prepare the way by air attack and ship bombardment for the land forces to take the enemy installations. In mid June the Japanese fleet made an attempt to stop the U.S. forces with wave after wave of Japanese dive bombers and torpedo bombers, 450 all. It failed miserably and suffered heavy losses in ships and planes in the Battle of the Philippine Sea.

By fall, the *Washington* and the carrier task group lay in full sight of the coast of Luzon in the Philippines. In January, they entered the South China Sea and attacked Saigon and Hong Kong. In February, 1945, came raids on Tokyo. They bombarded Iwo Jima in the days before the Marine landing.

In all, the *Washington* served 34 months in the Pacific. She damaged three enemy cruisers, a destroyer, and sank a battleship, destroyer, oil tanker and several transports. She shot down 12 enemy planes and bombarded 10 enemy islands. She steamed 289,609 miles during World War II and repelled 53 air attacks. She fired 3,535 rounds of 16-inch shells, 28,062 rounds of 5-inch projectiles and over 350,000 rounds of 20mm machine gun bullets. She earned 15 battle stars and was never hit, nor lost a man in battle action. She sank more combat tonnage than any U.S. battleship in World War II.

And, she was obsolete. Battleships were designed primarily for bombardment of shore installations prior to invasion by troops. New airplanes with longer ranges and heavier payloads, along with missiles in the years ahead, would largely replace the battleship. The *Washington* was scrapped in the 1960s. Its foot-thick steel armor would have a second life as part of a radioactive shield at the Brookhaven National Laboratory.

[1]Film star Dorothy Lamour was considered the epitome of an island girl with her long dark hair and flowered sarong, as she was pictured on the posters for the movie Road to Singapore

[2]Mel kept a list of ships in their task force, with name and number. BB stood for battleship, DD-destroyer, C for cruiser, AA for antiaircraft cruiser. He later went back to note which were sunk or damaged.

[3]Joe is slang for coffee.

[4]Musicant, Ivan, *Battleship at War—The Epic Story of the USS Washington*, Harcourt Brace Jovanovich, 1985, p. 90.

[5]Ibid, p. 121

[6] Bougainville Express, another name for the Tokyo Express. Bougainville is an island on the northern edge of the Solomon Island chain.

[7]Hari-carried is a slang term for committed suicide.

[8]Head is a Navy term for the bathroom.

Epilogue

When the war was over, Mel was offered the highest rank possible for an enlisted man, Warrant Officer. Two months short of four years in the Navy, he had enough. He had joined the Navy to see the world, but as he remarked with a grin "All I saw was water." He was ready to head home. But, since he had joined up and boarded ship on the east coast, he had to be discharged there. So once again, he rode through the Panama Canal, this time on a destroyer. And like his first day on a ship, he got violently seasick in his last days as the "tin can" lurched through stormy seas in the Caribbean.

By late October, he was back in North Dakota, helping with the chores on the family farm. One day in the post office at Warwick, he met Marie Anderson. Marie had spent the war years in Michigan, living with her brother and his family and working as "Rosie the Riveter," riveting together the leading edges on the wings of B24s, better known as the "Liberator."

Mel found the special friend he had wished for throughout his journal. The day before Thanksgiving in 1947, November 26, without fanfare, they were married by the minister at St. Olaf Lutheran Church in Devils Lake. That same fall, Mel found a house and some land, and was ready to go into farming and ranching with Marie at his side.

They missed the first reunions of the ships' crews. Often the reunions were during harvest time in central North Dakota, and, they were just "too blamed busy." But as the years passed, they found the time. Mel met up with his old buddies and Marie met his past.

"Those Easterners are different," she said of many of the reunion go-ers, "but our group, oh we had a lot of fun."

The reunions attracted good crowds for the meals, the speakers, the tours of ships and Navy museums, and the sharing with old buddies. Tucked into Mel's scrapbook is one unsigned explanation of the importance of those reunions:

"What is it that binds combat veterans together? … You can go to a company picnic or a convention and you will not feel the same emotion in the air as when you attend a veteran's reunion. There isn't the 'Band of Brothers' feeling that is felt when combat buddies get together.

It is something beyond regular friendship. It is the knowing that 'You and they have been to hell and back.' It is the deep-rooted emotion that brings you together. It is the knowledge that when things were tough, you and your buddies stuck it out and lived through it all.

… When combat buddies meet, whether it is 10 or 40 years, it seems like yesterday. All of the memories begin to assemble in your mind, memories that you thought had been pushed back into the recesses of your memory bank. 'Whatever happened to…' and 'Remember when…'

You try not to let on that these old veterans mean a lot to you, but by the time the flag is furled, the bills paid and the car packed, there is a lump in your throat and a tear in your eye as you part company with the men who once lived and fought beside you.

You tell your wife: 'Damn, it was good to see them again.' And it was! Yes, memories flood your mind as you head for home. No one knows the feelings except those of us who were there. You wonder if you will see any of them again. Combat was hell and you may have many terrible memories of death and destruction, but the memory of total camaraderie with men who shared that hell will forever be embedded in your heart. There is no friendship like that of combat buddies. It is something that lasts forever..."

It was at one of those reunions in the 1980s that Mel saw the notice that Ivan Musicant was looking for memoirs, diaries, journals, for the history he was writing on the *Washington*. Mel went down to the basement, where for 40 years the box had been stored with his journal and a collection of magazine articles, orders of the days, papers and memorabilia. Musicant described the package he got in the mail as "Christmas in July." He drew on Mel's journal for the book, along with the journals of several other sailors, memoirs of various officers as well as the ship's log and remaining "orders of the day."

About the same time, a group of Navy veterans in the Devils Lake area decided to start an annual "Dakota Bull Session" inviting Navy veterans to gather and swap memories, hearing from speakers and sharing some Navy meals, complete with beans. It was that group that learned of Mel's journal, and decided it ought to be published.

Sixty years later, Mel and Marie still go to ship reunions, although the group of buddies has dwindled to a handful. They live in the same house where they started their married life and raised their two children. Their son, Bradley runs the ranch. Bradley, his wife Sherry and son Calby live in a house across the road from Mel and Marie's. Their daughter, Sandra Hersrud, lives in Fargo with her husband Joe, and her son, Joshua Fossum. Her daughter, Heather Fossum, served for a year in Iraq with the 142nd National Guard.

Remember that silk that Mel wrote about buying during his brief shore leave when in the Caribbean? Marie went up in the attic and brought down two cardboard rolls with silk wrapped around them. He had bought three pieces of fabric. The pink one she had made into a blouse. The green and yellow were still there—60 years later. It had rode through the Pacific, through the tropics and the war in the bottom of Mel's seabag.

As he talked about the journal and those times, Mel leaned forward, and with typical Scandinavian seriousness, "Now, no bragging."

He leaned backed. "I didn't do anything heroic, nothing special. Now the Marines, the Army guys—they had it way tougher."

Did those guys ever give him a bad time about how easy the Navy guys had it?

"No," said Mel. "One of the fellows who was with the 164th on Guadalcanal lived about five miles from here. He says they were mighty
glad to see us out there. We circled around that island and bombarded it
several times."

So here it is. There aren't that many first person diaries on the war
around. With regulations forbidding them, only the determined, committed journalists kept writing. We've done light editing of Mel's penciled
journal—punctuation and paragraphs to make it easier to read, corrected
spellings here and there (but not everywhere), supplied a missing word
or two, and tried to make style elements such as capitalization consistent.
Occasionally his journal shifts abruptly—an indication that he had to
go, or someone came upon him. Today, some of his language would be
considered offensive or politically incorrect (but remarkably little). We
left it. It is a record of the way people spoke during the war. We've added
the historical context so the reader might understand the importance of
this journal's glimpse of history—of one man's navy.

—SRS